Internets, Intranets, and Extranets: New Waves in Channel Surfing

Internets, Intranets, and Extranets: New Waves in Channel Surfing has been co-published simultaneously as *Journal of Marketing Channels*, Volume 9, Numbers 3/4 2002.

The *Journal of Marketing Channels* Monographic "Separates"

Below is a list of "separates," which in serials librarianship means a special issue simultaneously published as a special journal issue or double-issue *and* as a "separate" hardbound monograph. (This is a format which we also call a "DocuSerial.")

"Separates" are published because specialized libraries or professionals may wish to purchase a specific thematic issue by itself in a format which can be separately cataloged and shelved, as opposed to purchasing the journal on an on-going basis. Faculty members may also more easily consider a "separate" for classroom adoption.

"Separates" are carefully classified separately with the major book jobbers so that the journal tie-in can be noted on new book order slips to avoid duplicate purchasing.

You may wish to visit Haworth's Website at . . .

http://www.HaworthPress.com

. . . to search our online catalog for complete tables of contents of these separates and related publications.

You may also call 1-800-HAWORTH (outside US/Canada: 607-722-5857), or Fax 1-800-895-0582 (outside US/Canada: 607-771-0012), or e-mail at:

getinfo@haworthpressinc.com

Internets, Intranets, and Extranets: New Waves in Channel Surfing, edited by Audhesh Paswan, PhD (Vol. 9, No. 3/4, 2002). *Examines the signaling cues essential to twenty-first century marketing channels.*

Franchising: Contemporary Issues and Research, edited by Patrick J. Kaufmann, PhD, and Rajiv P. Dant, PhD (Vol. 4, No. 1/2, 1995). *"An invaluable source of information for anyone doing research in the franchising field–a must review before developing your own research paradigms. . . . A collection of information and knowledge that no franchise executive should be without."* (Robert T. Justis, PhD, *Professor, Department of Management, Louisiana State University*)

Japanese Distribution Channels, edited by Takeshi Kikuchi, PhD (Vol. 3, No. 3, 1995). *"Gives an inside look at a topic that is often mysterious to business outside Japan. Kikuchi explains the historical reasons for the specialized channel system in Japan, as well as how the power has shifted from wholesalers to manufacturers in modern times. He also explains how the Japanese rebate system tends to support exclusive relationships with wholesalers."* (Market: AsiaPacific)

Wholesale Distribution Channels: New Insights and Perspectives, edited by Bert Rosenbloom, PhD (Vol. 3, No. 1, 1994). *"Current, topical, useful series of chapters beneficial to a practical understanding of the various facets and nuances of wholesale distribution channels. Readers will find the excellent treatment of sales force effectiveness by Adel El-Ansary worth the price of the book."* (Jay A. Smith, Jr., *Alabama Eminent Scholar of Industrial Distribution, Holder of Ben S. Weil Endowed Chair, School of Business/Graduate School of Management, University of Alabama*)

Direct Selling Channels, edited by Bert Rosenbloom, PhD (Vol. 2, No. 2, 1993). *Here is the first book to examine direct selling–the distribution of consumer products and services through personal, face-to-face sales away from fixed business locations.*

Internets, Intranets, and Extranets: New Waves in Channel Surfing

Audhesh Paswan
Editor

Internets, Intranets, and Extranets: New Waves in Channel Surfing has been co-published simultaneously as *Journal of Marketing Channels*, Volume 9, Numbers 3/4 2002.

Routledge
Taylor & Francis Group

LONDON AND NEW YORK

Internets, Intranets, and Extranets: New Waves in Channel Surfing has been co-published simultaneously as *Journal of Marketing Channels*, Volume 9, Numbers 3/4 2002.

First published 2002 by The Haworth Press, Inc.

2 Park Square, Milton Park, Abingdon, Oxfordshire OX14 4RN
605 Third Avenue, New York, NY 10017

Routledge is an imprint of the Taylor & Francis Group, an informa business

First issued in hardback 2020

Cover design by Marylouise E. Doyle

Library of Congress Cataloging-in-Publication Data

Internets, intranets, and extranets : new waves in channel surfing /
Audhesh Paswan, editor.
     p. cm. – (The journal of marketing channels monographic separates)
     "Co-published simultaneously as Journal of marketing channels, volume 9, numbers 3/4 2002."
     Includes bibliographical references and index.
     ISBN 0-7890-2010-6 (hard : alk. paper) – ISBN 0-7890-2011-4 (pbk : alk. paper)
     1. Marketing channels. 2. Internet. 3. Intranets (Computer networks) 4. Extranets (Computer networks) 5. Grazing (Television) 6. Internet marketing. 7. Electronic commerce. I. Paswan, Audhesh. II. Series.

HF5415.129 .I58 2002
658.8'02–dc21

            2002012417

ISBN 978-0-7890-2010-9 (hbk)

Indexing, Abstracting & Website/Internet Coverage

This section provides you with a list of major indexing & abstracting services. That is to say, each service began covering this periodical during the year noted in the right column. Most Websites which are listed below have indicated that they will either post, disseminate, compile, archive, cite or alert their own Website users with research-based content from this work. (This list is as current as the copyright date of this publication.)

(continued)

Special Bibliographic Notes related to special journal issues (separates) and indexing/abstracting:

- indexing/abstracting services in this list will also cover material in any "separate" that is co-published simultaneously with Haworth's special thematic journal issue or DocuSerial. Indexing/abstracting usually covers material at the article/chapter level.
- monographic co-editions are intended for either non-subscribers or libraries which intend to purchase a second copy for their circulating collections.
- monographic co-editions are reported to all jobbers/wholesalers/approval plans. The source journal is listed as the "series" to assist the prevention of duplicate purchasing in the same manner utilized for books-in-series.
- to facilitate user/access services all indexing/abstracting services are encouraged to utilize the co-indexing entry note indicated at the bottom of the first page of each article/chapter/contribution.
- this is intended to assist a library user of any reference tool (whether print, electronic, online, or CD-ROM) to locate the monographic version if the library has purchased this version but not a subscription to the source journal.
- individual articles/chapters in any Haworth publication are also available through the Haworth Document Delivery Service (HDDS).

Internets, Intranets, and Extranets: New Waves in Channel Surfing

CONTENTS

ABOUT THE EDITOR

Audhesh Paswan is Assistant Professor of Marketing at the University of North Texas. He earned his PhD in Marketing at the University of Mississippi (1992). Dr. Paswan also holds a Masters in Business Administration (MBA) from Indian Institute of Management, Ahmedabad, and a BTech from Indian Institute of Technology, Madras. His research interests include franchise management, relationalism, channel management, international marketing, and marketing pedagogy. His research has appeared in *Journal of Retailing, Journal of Business Research, Journal of Public Policy and Marketing, Journal of Business and Industrial Marketing, Journal of Entrepreneurial Behavior & Research, Asia Pacific Journal of Marketing and Logistics,* and *World Franchise & Business Report.* Before entering academe, he worked in the advertising and consumer product industries, managing sales, major accounts, products and research.

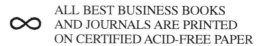

Introduction:
The e.Volution of the Spider

A noiseless, patient spider,
I mark'd, where, on a little promontory, it stood, isolated;
Mark'd how, to explore the vacant, vast surrounding,
It launch'd forth filament, filament, filament, out of itself;
Ever unreeling them–ever tirelessly speeding them.

–Walt Whitman, "A Noiseless Patient Spider"

Marketing channels are increasingly characterized by a complex web of linkages between people, places and processes. However, the spider web's delicate filaments are being displaced by Internet-enabling rugged fiber optics that create virtual connectedness between buyers and sellers. The fibers are communication conduits, but the message is often lost in the transmission. Channel members are seemingly navigating a web of coordinates in a vacant, vast surrounding. If these fiber optics are so enduring, why do so many Web-connected buyers and sellers remain disconnected? The virtual isolation in e.Mergent marketing channels addresses the embryonic stage of the e.Volution of Web-enabled technologies.

Channel members in this vacant, vast Web environment may be likened to the spider and the fly. Spiders know better than to venture to the outer circles of their webs. Instead, the patient spider settles in the center of the web, waiting for a vibration that signals where the fly can be "captured." There is an interplay between the captor and the captive that

[Haworth co-indexing entry note]: "Introduction: The e.Volution of the Spider." Pelton, Lou E. Co-published simultaneously in *Journal of Marketing Channels* (Best Business Books, an imprint of The Haworth Press, Inc.) Vol. 9, No. 3/4, 2002, pp. 1-2; and: *Internets, Intranets, and Extranets: New Waves in Channel Surfing* (ed: Audhesh Paswan) Best Business Books, an imprint of The Haworth Press, Inc., 2002, pp. 1-2. Single or multiple copies of this article are available for a fee from The Haworth Document Delivery Service [1-800-HAWORTH, 9:00 a.m. - 5:00 p.m. (EST). E-mail address: getinfo@haworthpressinc.com].

creates market vibrations; these vibrations are the signaling cues in the technological environment.

Today's channel spiders are like Black Widows: they spin webs that lack shape and form. While their webs appear erratic, the silk is stronger than other arachnids. The Black Widows are not aggressive, but they will react when disturbed. And, one must remember that the venom of the Black Widow is fifteen times as toxic as the venom of a prairie rattlesnake. These channel spiders potentially have a venomous impact on systemic flows of information, products and services.

Audhesh Paswan, editor of this special volume, and Lou E. Pelton have expertly selected a collection of manuscripts that address the signaling cues in 21st century marketing channels. The first set of articles focus on the channel member as Web-captor. The lead article by Bello et al. presents a framework of e-business technologies. The authors introduce the mediating role of channel structure on technology's impact on channel performance. Channel performance is also investigated in agency relationships, where sales representatives are faced with new technologies that foster channel disintermediation. Tamilia et al. explore the transaction cost underpinnings of cybermediaries, a role precipitated by Web-enabled environments. Griffith and Gray extend cue utilization theory as an explanatory mechanism for the Web-captive consumer. Finally, Mols provides an integrative investigation of the channels exosystem and Internet-based marketing channels.

Will the fly be lured by new technologies? I hope this volume provides both descriptive and prescriptive insights into a web of new e.Mergent channel paths: internets, intranets and extranets.

Lou E. Pelton
Editor

e-Business Technological Innovations: Impact on Channel Processes and Structure

Daniel C. Bello
Talai Osmonbekov
"Frank" Tian Xie
David I. Gilliland

SUMMARY. Modern distribution is being shifted from paper-based, people-intensive marketing systems toward electronic-based procedures that rely on Internet communications and web-enhanced software tools. This article develops a typology of e-business technological innovations that have come to characterize cutting-edge distribution management. e-Business tools relevant to marketing channels are organized by the channel process flows that yield communication and transaction enhancements to distribution systems. Further, a model of the impact of e-business on channel performance is developed. The mediating role of channel structure on technology's impact on channel outcomes in terms of efficiency and effectiveness is also analyzed. Finally, implications of the e-business revolution for managers and researchers are discussed. *[Article copies available for a fee from The Haworth Document Delivery Service: 1-800-HAWORTH.*

Daniel C. Bello is RoundTable Research Professor, Department of Marketing, Georgia State University Atlanta, GA 30303 (E-mail: dbello@gsu.edu). Talai Osmonbekov and "Frank" Tian Xie are Doctoral Candidates, Georgia State University. David I. Gilliland is Assistant Professor, Department of Marketing, Colorado State University.

Address correspondence to Daniel C. Bello.

[Haworth co-indexing entry note]: "e-Business Technological Innovations: Impact on Channel Processes and Structure." Bello, Daniel C. et al. Co-published simultaneously in *Journal of Marketing Channels* (Best Business Books, an imprint of The Haworth Press, Inc.) Vol. 9, No. 3/4, 2002, pp. 3-25; and: *Internets, Intranets, and Extranets: New Waves in Channel Surfing* (ed: Audhesh Paswan) Best Business Books, an imprint of The Haworth Press, Inc., 2002, pp. 3-25. Single or multiple copies of this article are available for a fee from The Haworth Document Delivery Service [1-800-HAWORTH, 9:00 a.m. - 5:00 p.m. (EST). E-mail address: getinfo@haworthpressinc.com].

3

KEYWORDS. e-Business, channel process flows, channel structure, channel performance

e-Business tools have the potential to revolutionize the efficiency and effectiveness of interfirm relationships in channels of distribution. Modern application software can speed the flow of information, automate inventory replenishment cycles, facilitate orders/payments, and otherwise enhance the performance of trading arrangements between manufacturers, resellers, and end users. While the potential benefits of innovative technological tools on channel systems have been widely acclaimed (Kalakota and Robinson 1999), little research has examined the specific channel conditions that are necessary to ensure that e-business initiatives yield "bottom-line" performance. In particular, little is known about the need to redesign fundamental business processes between channel members in order for the benefits of high-technology applications to be fully realized.

This article examines the critical role played by channel structure in mediating the impact of e-business tools on channel performance. Utilizing insights from the channels literature and coordination theory, the article examines the need for manufacturers and resellers to adapt their interfirm operations and governance procedures to meet the exacting requirements of sophisticated business software. This perspective recognizes that e-business involves much more than just electronic buying and selling technologies:

> *e-business*, in addition to encompassing e-commerce, includes both front- and back-office applications that form the engine for modern business. e-Business is not just about e-commerce transactions; it's about redefining old business models, with the aid of technology, to maximize customer value. e-Business is the overall strategy, and e-commerce is an extremely important facet of e-Business. (Kalakota and Robinson 1999, p. 4)

This article attempts to make three contributions to our knowledge of the impact that e-business tools have on marketing distribution systems. First, a typology of e-business technological innovations is developed that links software applications to the underlying channel process flows that constitute the primary functions of distribution systems. This new conceptual framework organizes the often confusing array of computer programs, acronyms, and web start-ups that constitute the e-business landscape into an ordered arrangement which links distribution tasks and e-business tools to communication and transaction enhancements. Second, coordination theory is used to isolate the specific ways that software applications improve the coordination of interfirm task and resource dependencies that connect members of a channel and account for performance outcomes. Third, a conceptual model is developed that highlights the need for channel members to re-engineer their operations and governance to accommodate the requirements of e-business solutions. Four propositions are derived from this conceptualization that stress the mediating role of channel structure in e-business software deployment.

The article proceeds by detailing the relationship between e-business tools and underlying channel processes. Next, the structural role of interfirm operations and governance is discussed, and propositions are developed. Finally, implications for managers and researchers are offered.

e-BUSINESS TECHNOLOGY AND CHANNEL PROCESSES

Channel theorists (Coughlan, Anderson, Stern, and El-Ansary 2001) note that process flows such as physical, promotion, ordering, and other flows constitute the fundamental work performed by organizations in channel systems. Manufacturers, resellers, and users participate in these basic channel processes by investing in resources (warehouses, salesforces, etc.) and performing tasks (advertising, selling, etc.) that are necessary to move a product and its title from the point of production to the point of consumption. Table 1 identifies six fundamental work processes that channel members participate in, and lists several tasks and resources associated with each process flow (Stern, El-Ansary, and Coughlan 1996). Unfortunately, channel performance suffers when the resources contributed and tasks performed by adjacent members are poorly coordinated, resulting in a basic process being conducted in an ineffective or inefficient manner. For example, the physical flow of products is conducted ineffectively when reseller inventories run low resulting in stock-outs and lost sales because the manufacturer is un-

TABLE 1. e-Business Technological Innovations

Channel Process Flows with Associated Distribution Task and Resources	Innovative Technological Tools	Communication/Transaction Enhancements
Physical Flow Warehousing Routing Transportation Tracking	SAP Logistics; Planning, Forecasting, & Replenishment (PFR); Vendor Managed Inventory (VMI); Shipment Tendering	Better facilitated physical movement of goods, real time tracking of shipments, optimal routing and status notification
Payment Flow Sales Order Billing/Invoicing Cash Receipts Wire Transfers	Oracle Bill Presentation & Payment; I-payment; Peachtree World Wide Wallet; IBM WebSphere Payment Manager	Increased speed of payment, credits, and reversals, more accurate bill/invoice processing, and accelerated cash flow
Ordering Flow Specification Setting Purchase Order Billing/Invoicing Delivery Receipts Return Authorizations	SAP B2B Procurement I-Store Rodopi Billing Calico Configurator	Accurate order specification, increased lead time, reduced data reentry errors and delays, and paperless operations
Risking Flow Credit Application Credit Approval Factoring Monitoring	Promise to Be Available (PBA) Expert 9.1 I-gear (URLabs) diCarta Contracts	Reduced inventory, credit, financial, contractual, and regulatory risks, enabled real time adjustments
Promotion Flow Promotion Planning Sales Management Coupons, Rebates Trade Show Planning	eLeads (Marketsoft); PRM Lead Management (Channelwave); I-Store; E-bate; Expo-Exchange; 3MC; Co-opLink	More efficient lead management, streamlined incentive process, increased promotional effectiveness, and more integrated coordination in planning
Negotiation Flow Negotiable Deals Asking Price Bidding Price Counter Offers Finalized Deals	eOffers (Marketsoft) PRM (Channelwave) LendingTree.com diCarta Contracts	Improved contract negotiation and management, new forms of many-to-many, many-to-one negotiations, and reverse auctioning

aware of downstream inventory levels and fails to ship replenishment stock in time.

From a coordination theory (Crowston 1997) perspective, poor channel performance of basic processes is due to the inadequate management of the dependencies existing among the tasks and resources. More specifically, the coordination links between those tasks and resources may not be well defined. Theorists define coordination as "managing dependencies between activities" (Malone and Crowston 1994, p. 90). Within a channel, it is the interdependencies among the distribution resources provided and tasks performed by firms that give rise to the need for coordination among channel actors (Alexander 1995). In this context, coordination is defined as the extent to which channel resources and tasks are conducted across the interfirm relationship in a consistent and coherent manner (Cheng 1983). The analysis of coordination between manufacturers and resellers requires examining "group action in terms of *actors* performing *interdependent activities* to achieve *goals*" (Crowston 1997, p. 159, emphasis in original). For example, a task-to-task dependency occurs when the success of a manufacturer's new product introduction activity is dependent on its reseller's selling activities. Such dependencies across organizations constrain how tasks can be performed and motivate the actors to engage in additional activities to overcome coordination problems.

Innovative Technological Tools

e-Business technology, most notably application software that automates various aspects of distribution processes, is a particularly potent coordination mechanism for channel systems. Sophisticated software package makers, such as SAP, Oracle, and IBM, are capitalizing on the benefit the Internet brings to e-business and offer complete business solutions that go beyond a firm's traditional boundary. These interfirm, web-based applications cover virtually all the functions performed by channel members but pose rigid demands on channel structure and coordination between channel members. For instance, SAP developed an open, collaborative business environment that incorporates existing SAP solutions into a web-enabled application: mySAP.com™. Users from the same organization can access the system anywhere using their personalized interface, and the system also provides access to a diverse group of web community members both upstream and downstream from the organization. The portal links market intelligence, product information, pricing, sales execution, order fulfillment, customer history, and customer relationship management together, even across platforms other than SAP's own. The smaller, more specialized software makers, such as Marketsoft and Channelwave, opt for the niche market with standalone programs that fit only certain tasks in the channel process. All such software provides a potential for better management of the dependencies between and among firms and marshal the resources utilized in the six channel process flows. To illustrate the potential impact of innovative e-business tools on channel flows and associated tasks within the flows, we provide examples and brief descriptions of popular software packages (see Table 1).

Physical Flow involves shifting the possession of products in sequence from producers through resellers and on to end users. To facilitate this process and associated tasks of warehousing, routing, transportation, and tracking, mySAP.com's Planning, Forecasting, and Replenishment (PFR) module enables channel members to collaborate on demand and supply, order quantity forecasting, and information exchange over the Internet. This innovation leads to optimal stock level for the buyers and reduced inventory for the supplier. The Vendor Managed Inventory (VMI) module, on the other hand, allows manufacturers to monitor the inventory level of wholesalers or retailers and proactively replenish orders on time and with greater accuracy. With the Shipment Tendering module in place, shippers and carriers can exchange detailed information about the pre-shipping bids, rates, conditions upon arrival, and real-time tracking. Importantly, less-than-truckload orders can be pooled and integrated through optimized freight movement and transportation exchange.

Payment Flow involves the transfer of payment backward from end users to resellers and on to manufacturers in exchange of the goods or services. A number of technological innovations have been developed to streamline the payment flow and the associated order initiation, invoicing, billing and fund transfer tasks. e-Business innovations enable actors in the channel to perform these tasks more accurately and efficiently. For example Oracle's Bill Presentment & Payment™ program uses an open-standards-based electronic billing and payment solution for business transactions. Another Oracle product, iPayment™, can accept payment instructions from almost any electronic commerce application and input payment data into a variety of financial and accounting systems. Traditional accounting software maker Peachtree developed Peachtree World Wide Wallet™ that enables merchants to accept credit card payments around the clock.

Ordering Flow and associated tasks such as setting specifications, purchase orders, billing and invoicing, delivery receipts, and return authorization are all characterized by heavy load of documentation and repeat entry of the same data into different systems of channel members. Calico's Configurator™ software enables online customers, partners and sales representatives to explore all possible options and easily customize even the most complex items on their purchase list. It also matches customer requirements with available product and service offerings in minutes. Similarly, SAP's B2B Procurement provides paperless operation and reduces data re-entry errors and resulting delays. Another billing/management software suite, Rodopi, features billing, bank reconciliation, customer support, e-mail to customers, on-line statements review and automated account setup on a variety of Unix and NT based servers.

Risking Flow in marketing channels involves the bearing and transferring of inventory risk, as well as other related credit, contractual, security, and regulatory risks. The associated tasks include credit application, credit approval, continuous monitoring, and factoring. mySAP.com's Promise to Be Available (PBA) supports dynamic sourcing and commitment of orders, taking into account information across production plants and distribution centers to match supply and demand. This greatly reduces the risk of one member of the channel having stock-outs or process delays. diCarta Contract helps channel members formulate, manage, and maintain the terms and clauses in the contract so that no contractual obligation will be overlooked by the involved parties.

Promotional Flow normally goes from the manufacturers to resellers and on to end users. Promotion planning, sales management, coupons, and rebates are major tasks and resources associated with the promotional flow. On-line couponing and rebating, such as I-Store modules, greatly simplify the process and reduce the cost of attracting customers. Both eLeads™ (by Marketsoft) and PRM Leads Management™ (by Channelwave) enable firms to optimize the flow of leads–getting qualified leads to the right people at the right time, and making measuring follow-up results simple. eLeads™ can also be used to manage leads across various dispersed departments and divisions of an organization.

Negotiation Flow is often the most ambiguous to examine and handle. Tasks and resources involved in the negotiation flow include negotiable deals to start with; offers to sell with asking price; offer to purchase with counter or bid price; forward and backward going counter offers; and deals that may be finalized. Web-enabled technological innovations can completely change the landscape of traditional negotiation process. More flexible, real-time, many-to-many, multilevel, and time and space independent negotiation formats and patterns become available. Online auctions and B2B exchanges such as Covisint enable instant buyer-seller interactions across the globe in a split second. Reverse auctions such as that of Lendingtree.com offer many-to-one customization of products and services that were unimaginable only a few years ago. Marketsoft's eOffers™ is a web-based offer-management and optimization solution that gives business executives the power to create, coordinate, and control promotions and negotiations for distribution to prospects and customers.

All the technological tools from the six channel flows categories enable firms to perform tasks and help allocate resources. Moreover, these tools are also reshaping the relationship between members. How these tools affect interfirm dependencies will now be discussed.

e-BUSINESS TOOLS AND INTERFIRM DEPENDENCE

As a guide to analyze organizational dependence, Crowston (1991) proposes a typology of dependencies and coordination mechanisms associated with those dependencies. Specifically, he divides dependencies into task-task, task-resource and resource-resource dependencies. Crowston (1997) builds upon previous preliminary typology and posits that coordination theory "is intended to analyze organizations in a way that facilitates redesign" (p. 161). Given the argument that companies are involved in a strategic redesign of their processes from traditional to e-business (Kalakota and Robinson 1999), we find coordination theory very suitable for the purposes of this paper.

Adopting Crowston's (1997) approach to classifying dependencies and recognizing temporal and spatial constraints of channel processes, we propose a matrix of channel process dependencies and dimensions of those dependencies. As discussed earlier, innovative technological tools may offer solutions to coordination problems in the respective channel process flows. The type and dimensions of channel process dependencies and respective e-business solutions to those dependencies are summarized in Table 2.

Task-to-Task Dependence: Task dependency occurs when two tasks share the same output (Malone and Crowston 1994). There are many tasks within channel flows that are characterized by various levels of dependence. We do not offer an exhaustive discussion of all tasks and activities, rather, we try to delineate some meaningful dimensions of

TABLE 2. Type and Dimensions of Dependency and e-Business Solutions[a]

Type of Dependency / Dimension	Task-to-Task	Task-to-Resource
Temporal	Tasks should be performed at same time; or the output of one task is input to another.	Resource is required by task; resource should be available at time task is performed.
Traditional:	Manufacturer develops leads and sends them by fax to reseller who calls on clients.	Local co-op advertising by retailers is self-reported and transmitted by fax to the manufacturer for payment.
e-Business:	**eLeads™** software package captures, qualifies and delivers leads to different channel members and measures results of the follow-up.	**Co-opLink™** software system captures co-op advertising information, facilitating approval and reimbursement procedures.
Spatial	Tasks should be performed at the same location; or tasks should provide inputs or outputs at same place.	Resource is required by a task; resource should be available at the same location task is performed.
Traditional:	Face-to-face contract negotiation sessions.	Sales rep visits client, providing expertise to configure complex order.
e-Business:	**diCarta Contracts™** provides online contract negotiation, registration and renewal; serves as a repository of all contracts and standardizes contract tracking.	**Calico Configurator™** enables client to configure complex order online, quickly meeting product requirements and compatibility constraints without leaving his/her office.

[a] Detailed explanations of the function, scope, and limitations of each e-business software package or module can be obtained at the web site of the program developer:
eLeads™ *http://www.marketsoft.com*
Co-opLink™ *http://www.coopcom.com*
diCarta Contracts™ *http://www.dicarta.com*
Calico Configurator™ *http://www.calicocommerce.com*

task-to-task dependency. As indicated in Table 2, there are two dimensions to this interdependence: temporal and spatial.

Temporal dimension of the task-to-task dependency refers to the necessity of actors to perform tasks in a certain time frame and sequence. In a traditional channel setting, overcoming the temporal dimension constraints may require considerable effort. Consider an OEM that generates substantial amount of sales leads during a tradeshow and now faces a task of passing them on to its suppliers. The leads need to be sorted according to the respective reseller territories and faxed to the resellers. The wait time between the manufacturer performing his task and the reseller being able to perform his is the coordination inefficiency that exists in a traditional channel. The advent of e-business tools offers an opportunity for the manufacturer to resolve the temporal inefficiency problems. Software packages such as eLeads™ offer a coordinating solution for the channel system. eLeads™ captures, qualifies and delivers leads by electronic means to different channel members depending on the type of lead at hand. The temporal inefficiency is reduced considerably with the deployment of this e-business tool as the lead development task and its delivery to the respective channel partner is for the most part automated.

Spatial dimension of the task-to-task dependency refers to the necessity of actors to perform tasks at the same location. Such binding dependency hinders timely contract negotiation and renewal tasks in a traditional channel setting as it is imperative for the parties to have face-to-face sessions at the same geographic location to sign a contract as an output of negotiations. Moreover, often several such meetings are necessary for the differences in views between the parties to be ironed out. In addition to contract content differences, often the arguments arise on the location of the next session, further disrupting the process of reaching an agreement. e-Business tools may offer coordinating solutions to such problems. For instance, diCarta Contracts™ is a software solution for contract management. It provides online contract negotiation, registration and renewal. The parties are no longer bound by the same location requirements as they can negotiate their contract clause by clause, paragraph by paragraph in front of their computers. Additionally, innovative companies may use videoconferencing, Lotus Notes and other similar tools to bridge spatial separation.

Task-to-Resource Dependence: Resource-to-task (task-to-resource) dependency occurs when a resource and a task share inputs and output (Malone and Crowston 1994). While the concept of channel tasks may be clear from our previous discussion, channel resources may need some explanation. Crowston's (1997) definition of resources includes everything used or affected by activities, including not only material goods but also the effort of actors. Thus, mission critical information, expertise, and equipment as well as personnel that are involved in activities can be considered a resource. Similar to task-to-task dependence, task-to-resource dependency exhibits two dimensions: temporal and spatial.

Temporal dimension refers to the necessity of a resource being available at the time a task is performed. In a traditional channel design, co-op advertising by retailers is often dependent on availability of co-op advertising funds provided by the manufacturer as well as the manufacturer's approval to use those funds. Under this arrangement, retailers often self-report co-op advertising information that is transmitted by fax for payment or reimbursement by the manufacturer. The wait time between manufacturer's approval (i.e., funds availability) and retailer's ability to perform co-op advertising task represents a coordinating inefficiency faced by the channel system in a traditional channel design. Importantly, slow approval and reimbursement procedures may lead to underutilization of designated co-op funds by intermediaries. e-Business channel design strategically deploys e-business tools to resolve such inefficiencies. For example, Co-opLink™ software system is designed to capture information pertaining to co-op advertising and facilitates approval and reimbursement procedures. Co-opLink™ provides the retailer with information on fund availability and ties together retailer's accruals and expenditures. The retailer no longer waits for the approvals to come through; information is available through a web site in real time that resolves this temporal task-to-resource dependency.

Spatial dimension refers to the necessity of a resource being available at the same location a task is performed. Traditionally, when a client faces a problem of configuring a complex order, manufacturer's sales rep visits the client's location to provide expertise to accomplish the task. This setup of a traditional channel system imposes a heavy strain on manufacturer's sales force, demanding a heavy travel schedule and maintenance of large in-house salesforce. Companies increasingly use call centers to advise clients over the phone. However, call centers have produced mixed results amid growing client complaints of time wasted being on hold and constantly interacting with unskilled phone operators (Hulme 2000). Clearly, clients are dependent on the manufacturer's specialized knowledge of its products in their task of placing a complex order. e-Business channel design, through implementation of e-business tools, can resolve spatial task-to-resource dependency at hand. Consider Calico Configurator™ software package that is geared to ease build-to-order manufacturing and complex ordering of electronics and computer systems. Calico Configurator™ enables clients to configure orders online simultaneously meeting compatibility constraints and product requirements. Calico Configurator™ produces 98.7% accurate orders and resolves spatial task-to-resource dependency as it relieves salespeople of the need to travel to the client's location.

Hence, e-business software tools address resource and task dependencies between channel members in the sense that "coordination in interorganizational systems acts to control and integrate work activity across organizational boundaries" (Alter 1990, p. 483). That is, resolving interfirm dependencies "is the process of concerting the decisions and actions of organizations, for a purpose or understanding that could not be accomplished by any one organization acting alone" (Alexander 1995, p. 67). However, the utilization of e-business software by channel members does not automatically improve distribution efficiency and effectiveness in some deterministic fashion. In fact, the mere adoption of software, *per se*, is unlikely by itself to enhance channel outcomes. Rather, the channel structure that organizes and manages the interactions of firms typically must be redesigned to accommodate and exploit the potential of e-business software.

e-BUSINESS TECHNOLOGY AND CHANNEL STRUCTURE

Robicheaux and Coleman (1994) note that the structure of a channel relationship consists of two dimensions: operational design and governance structure. The *operational design* of a channel refers to whether the tasks and resources of each member are independent and separate from those of its partner or whether the tasks and resources of the firms are combined and integrated. Operations can range from interfirm exchanges that are discrete (i.e., each partner operates autonomously) to those that are highly integrated (i.e., partners' operations are united or fused). The discrete-integrated continuum represents the economic arrangement of the channel since operations can be performed at the individual or system level, reflecting the degree of joint action undertaken by channel members.

e-Business technological innovations impact the operational design of a channel system by increasing the degree to which the tasks and resources of members need to be integrated. In particular, the proper utilization of software requires the integration of channel operations in terms of greater formalization, standardization, and centralization (see

Figure 1). Day-to-day operations between the partners become more formalized since software requires tasks and resources to take on a certain, definite pre-subscribed form. As O'Callaghan, Kaufmann and Konsynski (1992) observe, more compatible channel members' technological systems as well as business operations produce greater likelihood of adopting a technological innovation. Importantly, empirical findings by O'Callaghan et al. (1992) suggest that technological innovation adoption is associated with more intertwined business operations and ultimately the increased volume of transactions between the firms.

An example of an e-business tool requiring explicit, formal operations between channel partners is IBM's WebSphere line of e-business packages. This retail-oriented bill presentation and payment module requires connected channel members to process payments, reversals, and credits in a pre-formatted, step-by-step procedure. Also, greater integration is reflected by additional standardization (of inputs, activities, and outputs) of the tasks and resources employed by partners that utilize an e-business tool. That is, interfirm operations are brought into conformity with software requirements. For example, Southwest Airlines announced that it will use WebSphere platform to standardize its business operations across its supplier and customers. Finally, operations become integrated in the sense that tasks and resources become centralized. When Fruit of the Loom decided to establish an electronic link

FIGURE 1. The Impact of e-Business on Channel Performance: The Mediating Role of Channel Structure

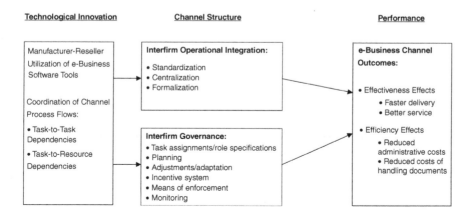

with its distributors, the company invested in the centralized web site as well as underwriting distributors' investments in web servers to access the central database of transactions (Kosiur 1997). Thus, operations are concentrated or focused by considering work centrally, at the group level of all members, superseding the dispersed or scattered efforts formerly exercised by individual members. To summarize, the following proposition can be stated:

- Proposition 1: e-business technological innovations affect interfirm operational integration by requiring:

  a. increased formalization,
  b. increased standardization,
  c. increased centralization.

The changes that follow or must be undertaken while adopting technological tools in marketing channels have been studied in previous research. O'Callaghan, Kaufmann and Konsynski (1992) note that technological tools produce changes not only in internal economy but also in internal polity of the channel system. Physical integration of the partner firms' systems is an important issue in terms of implementation time, compatibility, etc., but even a more pressing issue becomes how firms integrate their basic business operations in order for the software to work to its potential for the benefit of both firms.

In contrast to operations, the *governance design* of a channel refers to the way decisions about the tasks and resources associated with a channel system are made (Heide 1994). The decision-making process can range from unilateral (i.e., one member makes choices) to bilateral (i.e., both members collaborate on choices). The unilateral-bilateral continuum represents the polity arrangement of the channel since decisions can be fully administered by an individual member or they can be shared equally. Thus, the governance continuum reflects the degree of participation and shared decision-making involved in resolving choices about channel tasks and resources. Governance theorists (Heide 1994) identify six governance activities in which members engage in order to make decisions about channel issues (see Figure 1). From an e-business perspective, the first three governance activities–role specification, planning, and adjustments–are crucial to resolving choices during the pre-implementation stage of software deployment.

Role specification refers to the manner in which tasks and resources are assigned to each of the exchange partners. For instance, Chrysler unilaterally required its suppliers to participate in its EDI network and mandated the adoption of protocols and standards (Steinfeld, Kraut, and Plummer 1998). Chrysler management felt that this type of *en force* requirement for the upstream channel members was justified by the company's drive to reap the efficiencies of electronic transactions. Similarly, General Electric's decision to sever relationships with the suppliers who don't adopt web transactions suggests the unilateral approach for the role specification in the pre-implementation phase of software deployment. In contrast, Fruit of the Loom deployed an integrated network with its distributors on a bilateral, collaborative basis by working together with them on developing an interactive database, catalog, and ordering system over the web that met their mutual needs (Kosiur 1997).

Planning refers "to the process by which future contingencies and consequential duties and responsibilities in a relationship have been made explicit ex ante" (Heide 1994, p. 76). An example of a unilateral planning process would be the elaborate franchise contracts that give the franchiser broad, unilateral planning powers over the business strategy that will be utilized by franchisees in the system. So if a large chain of franchised businesses would undertake an e-business initiative the planning process would most likely come from the franchisor. On the other hand, under bilateral governance, the parties are most likely to plan adoption of e-business tools in consultations with each other. For instance, in the Fruit of the Loom case the company and its distributors jointly planned the interactive web system in the absence of a formal contract or specific deadlines for the completion of their e-business project (Kosiur 1997).

Adjustment refers to the process used to decide on the changes and adaptations that may be required as a software deployment is implemented. Under bilateral governance, the parties flexibly negotiate adjustments in response to environmental changes or unexpected problems. When Fruit of the Loom distributors expressed a concern about the cost of the web server architecture and middleware, the company decided to adjust its plans and bear the cost of the enabling technologies. This type of response to a partner's concern illustrates the bilateral nature of adjustments made by the Fruit of the Loom. Alternatively, the Chrysler EDI rollout was unilaterally administered by the auto manufacturer and Chrysler's information technology specialists adapted the protocols to Chrysler's evolving requirements (Steinfeld, Kraut, and Plummer 1998). As this case illustrates, the adjustments were made only to one party's benefit, exemplifying a unilateral nature of adjustment process. As stated earlier, the three processes discussed are thought to be more important in the software implementation stage and may be carried out both in bilateral as well as unilateral fashion. So, we offer the following proposition:

- Proposition 2: e-business technological innovations affect interfirm governance in terms of role specification, planning, and adjustments being most important during the software's pre-implementation phase.

The final three governance activities–incentives, monitoring, and enforcement–are critical to making decisions after the software has been deployed. During the post-implementation phase, ongoing decisions must be made to maintain the integrity of the e-business solution adopted by the parties. As Merchant (1988) observes, such governance involves "the back end of the management process where managers attempt to ensure that things are going the way they should" (p. 40).

Incentives involve the inducements that encourage the parties to behave in a particular fashion. Unilaterally, the more powerful party may motivate desired actions by rewarding or penalizing certain behaviors of its partner. From an e-business perspective, one would expect GE to offer monetary or other incentives to the suppliers who continuously utilize GE's web interface and banning the suppliers who may try to sabotage by transacting in the traditional fashion. Under a bilateral approach, incentives are tied to a lesser extent to specific performance but depend on the display of system-relevant attitudes and behaviors. For instance, retailers were motivated to participate in e-business solutions (electronic order tracking and fulfillment) maintained by Sony of Canada because of their allegiance and identification with this prestigious multinational corporation (Roche and O'Connel 1998). This case illustrates the point made by Simon (1991) and reiterated by Heide (1994): ". . . in a purely bilateral system, the identification with the system represents a reward in its own right" (p. 77).

Monitoring procedures are the surveillance systems used for gathering and evaluating information. Under unilateral governance, the controlling party measures performance outcomes to insure proper contractual compliance (Anderson and Oliver 1987). The deployment of e-business tools may substantially increase the transparency of the channel, greatly enhancing the unilateral monitoring capabilities of the partners. For instance, Fujitsu Computer Products and 3Com Corporation have exploited this opportunity by pushing their channel partners for higher sales, aided by their enhanced ability to measure and analyze complex sales data (Marchetti 1999). Bilateral monitoring is often expressed in self-monitoring, when the parties understand their responsibilities through socialization processes. From an e-business perspective, bilateral monitoring process may be enhanced since increased interfirm communications enabled by the e-business tools (Boyle and Alwitt 1999) could further lead to enhanced socialization activities.

Enforcement means involve methods employed for compelling compliance with a particular course of action. Unilateral enforcement relies on explicit, legitimate authority specified in contractual agreements. For example, USWeb Corporation relies on its long-term franchise agreements with web developers and software integrators to obtain their compliance with its programs (Kanellos 1996). Under the bilateral governance, the parties rely on informal social pressure from relational norms to direct behavior of partners. Because of the relational norms and expected future interactions, firms are likely to manifest "forbearance" and the need for specific enforcement mechanisms is low (Heide 1994). From an e-business perspective, self-control could be enhanced as e-business tools provide the means to evaluate the mutual benefits of an exchange. For instance, Fruit of the Loom distributors realized the benefits of the electronic transactions after the pilot program, however they did not fully integrate their ordering systems in time. Fruit of the Loom demonstrated flexibility in enforcing the distributors' contractual obligations, and "forbore" the inefficiencies in the system until the distributors finished standardizing their ordering and fulfillment systems.

To summarize, the following proposition reflects the expected relationship between the adoption of e-business tools and channel governance:

- Proposition 3: e-business technological innovations affect interfirm governance in terms of incentive system, means of enforcement, and monitoring being most important during the software's post-implementation phase.

MEDIATING ROLE OF STRUCTURE ON CHANNEL PERFORMANCE

The Figure 1 model of the impact of e-business on channel performance posits that interfirm operational integration and governance directly antecede the effectiveness and efficiency effects of software on the channel. Consistent with theoretical notions of channel structure (Robicheaux and Coleman 1994), the structural dimensions of operations and governance are modeled as determinants of channel performance outcomes. In contrast, the utilization of e-business tools is shown to directly impact the requirements for interfirm operations and governance but only indirectly affecting channel performance. That is, the ability of channel members to achieve the necessary reengineering of operations and governance is viewed as mediating the effect of e-business tools on performance.

To the extent firms in a channel relationship are unsuccessful in integrating their operations, their adoption of e-business software is unlikely to yield the anticipated performance enhancements. For software to improve distribution efficiency and effectiveness, firms must standardize, centralize and formalize their operations, enabling the software to coordinate the task and resource dependencies it was designed to address. For instance, Co-opLink requires manufacturers and resellers to organize and manage their advertising activities (media and creative) in strict accordance with the software's data entry and reporting requirements. The wholesale drug distributor McKesson had to integrate its operations with CVS retail chain to implement Continuous Replenishment Management (CRM) system. This includes sharing historical point-of-sale data on a store-by-store basis, operational plans and inventory stocking (Kalakota and Robinson 1999). More generally, trading partners must redesign their business operations in order to exploit the potential of e-business tools to coordinate business processes and enhance "bottom-line" performance. The following proposition summarizes this perspective.

- Proposition 4: The impact of e-business tools on channel performance is mediated by the ability of the trading partners to integrate their operations.

For software to coordinate channel processes effectively, firms must be prepared to make decisions regarding the tasks and resources they utilize to distribute products. Prior to implementing a software solution, the members must be able to specify their new roles, plan for future contingencies, and adjust to problems. Typically, if there is a strong power asymmetry in a channel, the more powerful party is likely to dominate the pre-deployment decision-making process. Under such unilateral choice procedures, acquiescence by the weaker party can enable the partners to deploy the e-business tools in a way that enhances performance. For example, power retailers such as Home Depot and Wal-Mart have achieved significant channel efficiencies by requiring their vendors to meet strict EDI and other software-related standards and procedures (Kalakota and Robinson 1999). On the other hand, if the channel is characterized by symmetry in member power, a collaborative bilateral decision-making process is likely. In terms of the on-going maintenance of software, the members must likewise develop either unilateral or bilateral decision procedures. Specifically, incenting, monitoring, and enforcing the choice process of channel members must be established to ensure the continued viability and effectiveness of an e-business tool.

Unfortunately, decision-making between channel members is not always productive because disagreements and conflict can erupt, crippling the ability of the parties to make effective decisions. While members are often cooperative, analysts observe that "the process of conflict, however, is pervasive and inherent in channel systems" (Rosenberg and Stern 1970, p. 70). The interdependence of member tasks and resources may give rise to conflict when one firm's actions are viewed as blocking or interfering with another's ability to perform its tasks (Jehn 1997). Task and resource dependencies can lead to tension and disputes between firms when the actions of one firm's managers impede or otherwise frustrate the activities of adjacent firms. For as Schmidt and Kochan (1972) state, firms may be "dependent upon one another during the activity stage for scheduling, compliance, or coordination of activities . . . [and the] interdependence of activity where goals are incompatible presents occasion for potential conflict" (p. 36).

The processes of installation and launch of new innovative technologies may exacerbate prior friction issues as well as create new domain divergence, different reality perceptions and goal incongruence, the sources of channel conflicts (Coughlan et al. 2001). For instance, one of the first issues the parties may disagree on would be the particular choice of the e-business platform. Many companies provide e-business application solutions with a wide variety of options available that make the ultimate choice an extremely important one. The decision process for such issues will determine the nature of the conflicts that may face the dyad. Importantly, dysfunctional disagreements can derail efforts to properly organize and manage the deployment and maintenance of software, greatly inhibiting the performance enhancements that potentially can flow from technological innovations. To summarize previous discussion we suggest the following proposition:

- Proposition 5: The impact of e-business tools on channel performance is mediated by the unilateral and bilateral governance activities of the trading partners.

DISCUSSION AND IMPLICATIONS

Manufacturers, resellers, and end users can gain greater effectiveness and efficiency in their exchange relationships through the adoption of e-business technologies. Recent breakthroughs in software design and the information technology infrastructure enable business partners to initiate, negotiate, consummate, and track exchanges faster and cheaper. While e-business tools have the potential to revolutionize relationships among members of the distribution channel, managers and researchers need to be alert to the demands that modern telecommunications, computer, video, and e-business technologies make on traditional business practices. This article has identified the linkages between sophisticated software, traditional channel processes, and the potential communication and transaction enhancements that can flow to channel participants. The article stresses that the ability of e-business tools to automate channel processes is constrained by the dependencies that link the tasks and resources of members. Consequently, managers and researchers must fully consider the role played by the structure of the channel in mediating the performance-enhancing qualities of contemporary software innovations.

Moreover, some researchers suggest that the network structure, in which the dyadic relationships are embedded, plays an important role (Anderson, Hakansson and Johanson 1994). This paper did not specifically address this issue. As e-business tools start to encompass the supply chains and even larger networks of businesses, the network perspective might shed light and help to gain additional insights into the nature of impact of e-business tools on marketing channels. Future research should undertake this important step of studying e-business developments from a network relationship perspective. While considering multiple supply chain electronic links through e-business tools, future researchers should keep in mind the problems with legacy systems and difficulties of incorporating them with the new e-business supply-chain design.

For managers, cutting-edge e-business tools represent an historical opportunity to add value to channel relationships in a way that benefits customers, partners, employees, and other stakeholders. For competitive reasons, firms cannot afford to ignore the potential increases in marketing effectiveness and efficiency that can follow the automation of key business processes. However, this article makes clear that managers charged with implementing e-business solutions must understand the fundamental impacts software can have on the temporal and spatial dependencies connecting the task and resources of firms up and down the channel. To exploit the ability of software to coordinate channel tasks and resources, managers need to accommodate the operations and governance activities that manage and organize exchange relationships. Such an accommodation involves the redesigning of many traditional industry and channel practices. Yet without fundamental adaptations to channel structure, managers are unlikely to achieve the speed and cost advantages associated with high technology innovations. As mentioned before, with high levels of technological innovations, there are often multiple software packages available in the market. In this situation, the cross platform compatibility becomes an important aspect for a firm's day-to-day operations. Our paper considers several leading packages that seem to generate well-publicized success stories in the industry practice. Managers should carefully examine the whole array of products available and choose the ones that best fit their specific needs and present with the most potential in their respective industries.

For researchers, the automation of business processes through technology has a profound effect on the way channel processes are conceptualized, modeled, and investigated. Traditional conceptualizations of the boundaries of channel institutions are challenged by modern software's abilities to heighten task and resource dependencies as well as to seamlessly integrate the operations of channel members. Operational integration can blur the boundaries between firms and even make distinctions between manufacturers and resellers less distinct during the distribution processes. Theorists have yet to integrate such transformational effects into the theory of the firm and the analysis of interorganizational relationships and behavior. Beyond theoretical conceptions, the most appropriate ways to model channel systems and investigate on-going channel processes are also challenged by the revolutionary impacts e-business tools can have on distribution systems. Empirical researchers may have to reassess their definitions and operationalizations of constructs as well as their research methodologies.

To conclude, current trends in software and information technology suggest that channel practices are likely to continue to evolve at a rapid rate. Cutting-edge practitioners will likely continue to employ technical innovations in ways that revolutionize the efficiency and effectiveness of marketing channel operations. Hence, researchers will be continually challenged to understand underlying processes and to offer robust models that capture the impact this technological juggernaut has on marketing.

REFERENCES

Alexander, Ernest R. (1995), *How Organizations Act Together: Interorganizational Coordination in Theory and Practice*. New York: Gordon and Beach.

Alter, Catherine (1990), "An Exploratory Study of Conflict and Coordination in Interorganizational Service Delivery Systems," *Academy of Management Journal*, 33 (3), 478-502.

Boyle, B. A. and Alwitt L. F. (1999), "Internet Use Within the U.S. Plastics Industry," *Industrial Marketing Management*, Vol. 28, pp. 327-341.

Coughlan, Anne T., Erin Anderson, Louis W. Stern and Adel I. El-Ansary (2001), *Marketing Channels*, 6th Edition, Upper Saddle River, NJ.

Cheng, Joseph L. C. (1983), "Interdependence and Coordination in Organizations: A Role-System Analysis," *Academy of Management Journal*, 26 (1), 156-162.

Crowston, Kevin (1991), "Towards a Coordination Cookbook: Recipes for Multi-Agent Action," Unpublished doctoral dissertation, Cambridge, MA: MIT Sloan School of Management.

Crowston, Kevin (1997), "A Coordination Theory Approach to Organizational Process Design," *Organization Science*, 8 (2), March-April, 157-175.

Heide, Jan B. (1994) "Interorganizational Governance in Marketing Channels," *Journal of Marketing*, 58 (1), 71-85.

Hulme, George V. (2000), "Help!" *Sales and Marketing Management*, February, 20-22.

Jehn, Karen A. (1997), "A Qualitative of Conflict Types and Dimensions in Organizational Groups," *Administrative Science Quarterly*, 42 (September), 530-557.

O'Callaghan, Ramon, Patrick J. Kaufmann and Benn R. Konsynski (1992) "Adoption Correlates and Share Effects of Electronic Data Interchange Systems in Marketing Channels," *Journal of Marketing*, 56 (2), pp. 45-56.

Kalakota, Ravi and Marcia Robinson (1999), *e-Business: Roadmap for Success*, Reading, MA: Addison-Wesley Inc.

Kanellos, Michael (1996), "Internet gives franchise concept new life," *Computer Reseller News*, 715, p. 59, 66, December 16.

Kosiur, David (1997), *Understanding Electronic Commerce*, Microsoft Press.

Malone, Thomas and Kevin Crowston (1994), "The Interdisciplinary Study of Coordination," *Computing Surveys*, 26, 1, 87-119.

Marchetti, Michele (1999), "Peace Offering," *Sales & Marketing Management*, 149 (10).

Merchant, Kenneth M. (1988), "Progressing Toward a Theory of Marketing Control: A Comment," *Journal of Marketing*, 52 (July), 40-44.

Robicheaux, Robert A. and James E. Coleman (1994), "The Structure of Marketing Channel Relationships," *Journal of the Academy of Marketing Science*, 22 (1), 38-51.

Roche, Karen and, Bill O'Connell (1998), "Dig a wider channel for your products," *Marketing News*, 32, 23, p. 10.

Rosenberg, Larry J. and Louis W. Stern (1970), "Toward the Analysis of Conflict in Distribution Channels," *Journal of Marketing*, 34 (October), 40-46.

Schmidt, Stuart M. and Thomas A. Kochlan (1972), "Conflict: Toward Conceptual Clarity," *Administrative Science Quarterly*, 19 (September), 359-370.

Simon, Herbert (1991), "Organizations and Markets," *Journal of Economic Perspectives*, 5, 25-44.

Steinfeld, Charles, Robert Kraut and Alice Plummer (1998), "The Impact of Interorganizational Networks on Buyer-Seller Relationships," *Journal of Computer Mediated Communications*, 1 (3), 1-15.

Stern, Louis W., Adel I. El-Ansary, and Anne T. Coughlan (1996), *Marketing Channels*, 5th edition, Englewood Cliffs, NJ: Prentice-Hall, Chapter 1 (pp. 1-33), pp. 192-199.

Conventional Channels of Distribution and Electronic Intermediaries: A Functional Analysis

Robert D. Tamilia
Sylvain Senecal
Gilles Corriveau

SUMMARY. The paper analyses electronic channel members using functional analysis and examines how such cybermediaries differ in the way they carry out the marketing functions or flows relative to conventional channel participants. Some electronic intermediaries are examined. Micro and macro issues dealing with the economics and politics of channels are also presented. Finally, a plea is made to know more about the business costs of transacting on the Internet. Such cost analyses will help determine the extent to which cybermediaries will supplant or complement traditional channels. *[Article copies available for a fee from The Haworth Document Delivery Service: 1-800-HAWORTH. E-mail address: <getinfo@haworthpressinc.com> Website: <http://www.HaworthPress.com> © 2002 by The Haworth Press, Inc. All rights reserved.]*

Robert D. Tamilia is Professor of Marketing, University of Quebec at Montreal. Sylvain Senecal is Assistant Professor of Ecommerce and Marketing, College of Business Administration, University of Toledo. Gilles Corriveau is Associate Professor of Marketing, École des Hautes Études Commerciales (affiliated with the University of Montreal).

Address correspondence to: Robert D. Tamilia, University of Quebec at Montreal, DSA, PO Box 6192 Downtown, Montreal QC H3C 4R2 Canada (E-mail: tamilia. robert@uqam.ca).

[Haworth co-indexing entry note]: "Conventional Channels of Distribution and Electronic Intermediaries: A Functional Analysis." Tamilia, Robert D., Sylvain Senecal, and Gilles Corriveau. Co-published simultaneously in *Journal of Marketing Channels* (Best Business Books, an imprint of The Haworth Press, Inc.) Vol. 9, No. 3/4, 2002, pp. 27-48; and: *Internets, Intranets, and Extranets: New Waves in Channel Surfing* (ed: Audhesh Paswan) Best Business Books, an imprint of The Haworth Press, Inc., 2002, pp. 27-48. Single or multiple copies of this article are available for a fee from The Haworth Document Delivery Service [1-800-HAWORTH, 9:00 a.m. - 5:00 p.m. (EST). E-mail address: getinfo@haworthpressinc.com].

KEYWORDS. Cybermediaries, electronic intermediaries, political economy

INTRODUCTION

The Internet represents many opportunities and challenges for organizations in this new millennium. It is a new and powerful information medium for producers, wholesalers and retailers to conduct business among each other, and with consumers as well. The Internet is not only a communication tool or an information system, it is also a marketplace as well as a distribution channel for certain types of products and services. By 2003, in the United States alone, the size of the e-commerce business-to-consumer market (B2C) and the business-to-business segment of the economy (B2B) are expected to reach $75 billion and $633 billion, respectively (International Data Corporation 1999).

Notwithstanding the current slow down in the economy, these numbers are indeed impressive. They represent a significant shift in the way business transactions are carried out in the economy. Moreover, specialized electronic channel intermediaries have emerged to carry out the work needed to handle the business generated in the so-called "new economy." In fact, marketing has yet to grasp the significance of these new electronic intermediaries. In spite of the growing importance of the Internet as a tool for the business community, little academic work exists in marketing that provide insights as to how this new technological medium for market transactions will affect traditional channel structure and relationships (Bailey and Bakos 1997).

For example, it is almost a truism (perhaps even a myth?) amongst enthusiastic Internet proponents that the number of channel intermediaries will decrease significantly (e.g., Libresco 1997). Anecdotal evidence offered by Gellman (1996) supporting disintermediation is typical. Moreover, Internet supporters have predicted that in-store retail sales will drop in favor of retail sales generated through the Internet. However, very little theoretical or empirical research exists to support such claims. Yet Keep and Hollander (1992) have shown that nonstore retailing, as a percentage of total retail sales, has not enjoyed sustained growth over the past one hundred years, and is unlikely to gain over traditional retail channels. Moreover, the percent of all nonstore retail sales relative to total retail sales (including direct marketing, telephone sales, TV shopping, etc.) has been less than three percent over the last several decades (even lower in Canada). Such historical data go against hyped predictions that 15%, 20% and even 50% of *all* retail sales will be done over the Internet in the not too distant future (e.g., *The Economist* 2000). This indicates a real need to better understand the functioning of traditional marketing channels and to see the extent to which electronic channels will supplant or complement them.

It is important that a solid conceptual understanding of the nature of channels of distribution be established at this early stage in order to more fully understand how the Internet will impact or affect the way traditional channels work. Channel theory will enable us to verify if such wild statements are theoretically sound, leading eventually to their empirical validation through hypothesis testing.

Thus, the basic objective of this paper is to examine how the Internet affects certain micro and macro issues dealing with the politics and economics of distribution channels. We will also compare and contrast the marketing functions or flows performed in a traditional channel with similar marketing work carried out using the Internet.

According to Palamountain (1955), all channels of distribution are both economic and political economic entities. Moreover, channels are embedded in a social structure that has been molded and shaped over time to reflect cultural and social values of the participants. These participants (i.e., buyers and sellers) have established economic and social relationships based on trust and power, which influence the way they do business with each other (Arndt 1983). Of course, electronic intermediaries are relatively new, and the same economic and environmental forces which shaped traditional channels will also influence their structure.

Moreover, using some of the concepts advanced by Stern and Reve (1980) in their proposed political economy framework, we explore some of the "critical dimensions determining the transactional effectiveness and efficiency in distribution" (page 52). We hope to demonstrate that the Internet has the potential to improve information-based marketing functions and flows compared to those performed in traditional channels. However, the micro and macro political analyses suggest that channel members, industry groups, and even governments need to monitor the Internet in order to avoid conflict and inequality between participating channel members. Consumers also need to be aware what Internet-based transactions mean for them if some of the economic efficiencies the Internet can provide are realized and be beneficial to them.

CYBERMEDIARIES AND MACRO ECONOMIC ISSUES

According to Stern, El-Ansary and Coughlan (1996), a distribution channel can be defined as a "set of interdependent organizations involved in the process of making a product or service available for consumption or use" (page 1). Hence, many intermediaries or resellers fall into this category of organizations. To illustrate the prominence of intermediaries on the Internet (also called "cybermediaries" or electronic intermediaries), Carr (2000) showed that the information search process resulting in a simple consumer purchase on the Internet can involve, directly or indirectly, as many as nine different cybermediaries (content providers, affiliate sites, search engines, portals, software makers, wholesalers, retailers, banks, postal services), each one receiving a share, albeit small, in the price paid by the consumer. Carr states that business is not experiencing disintermediation but rather "hypermediation" (i.e., more intermediaries), a conclusion shared by Bailey and Bakos (1997) in their case studies of firms involved in e-commerce.

The rise in the number of electronic intermediaries has also been supported by Sarkar, Butler and Steinfield (1995). Thus, more not less intermediaries seem to be created by the Internet, a conclusion that is the exact opposite of commonly accepted wisdom, especially by e-commerce aficionados. The new electronic intermediaries create value for consumers, producers, retailers, wholesalers, and other facilitating agents by providing economic utilities of time, place and possession (Shaw 1994). Let us not forget that the Internet also provides a means by which data from both suppliers and customers can be better managed for all parties concerned.

Such specialized electronic intermediaries (referred to by Sarkar, Butler and Steinfield 1995 as spot market makers, barter networks, directory service intermediaries, intelligent agents, gateways, search site providers, search service providers, virtual malls, financial intermediaries, web publishers, web site evaluators, virtual resellers, web auditors, web forums, fan clubs and user groups) are able to perform many business and marketing tasks that were solely performed before by more traditional intermediaries. According to Peterson, Balasubramanian and Bronneberg (1997), the Internet has some of the following characteristics and these no doubt foster the need for (specialized) electronic channel members to emerge in order to perform such cyber-work:

1. Ability to inexpensively store large amounts of information in multiple locations.

2. Availability of powerful and inexpensive tools to search, organize and communicate information.
3. Interactivity within and between organizations.
4. Ability to provide a new medium for communication.
5. Ability to serve as a transaction medium.
6. Ability to serve as a distribution medium for numeric goods.
7. Relatively low barriers of entry.

Many more such tasks could be added as argued by English (1985) or Sarkar, Butler and Steinfield (1995). Most marketing channel textbooks explain at great length the tasks assumed by conventional channel members (e.g., Stern, El-Ansary and Coughlan 1996; Pelton, Strutton and Lumpkin 1997). Suffice to say that in order to better understand how these tasks enable electronic channel members on the Internet to fully realize their value added potential, one needs to understand how marketing functions or marketing flows affect the structure and operational efficiency of the distribution of goods and services to businesses and consumers.

CYBERMEDIARIES AND MARKETING FUNCTIONS

Marketing channel scholars generally agree that marketing functions are indispensable and universal, and they must be performed somewhere by someone in the distribution structure in order for market exchanges to be realized (Beckman and Davidson 1967). Functional analysis in marketing states very clearly that marketing functions (i.e., the work needed to bring goods and services from points of production to points of consumption or utilization) cannot be eliminated, even if channel intermediaries can be circumvented.

By definition, marketing functions are not static. They are dynamic and can be performed by a member of the distribution channel at one point in time and subsequently transferred to a competitor or within the existing distribution channel (upstream or downstream the distribution chain) to a more efficient member (Mallen 1973). Moreover, the performance of marketing functions is subject to the entrepreneurial insights of channel members themselves, as well as the technological and legal forces that impact the way they are carried out in the channel.

The recent emergence of the Internet as a distribution channel has already given place to a process of disintermediation and reintermediation. No doubt many manufacturers first saw the opportunity to shorten their distribution channel and to sell directly to final customers or users. By doing so, cost savings were anticipated because the margins normally given to traditional intermediaries would now remain within the firm. However, by internalizing tasks that had been traditionally performed by outside channel agencies, manufacturers realized that their cost of performing such marketing functions were in fact higher than when these were "contracted out," as argued by Sarkar, Butler and Steinfield (1995). Such tasks as single item order management, promotional effort, supporting marketing research, product assortment services, and many other marketing services normally performed by traditional intermediaries were now the sole responsibility of manufacturers (Reda 1999; Alba et al. 1997; Stern, El-Ansary and Coughlan 1996).

Moreover, the cost of performing these marketing functions resulted in higher costs than when these were done by traditional channel members. No doubt manufacturers discovered at their own expense that the vertical integration of marketing functions was not such a simple task. Disintermediation led to a loss in efficiency by manufacturers. Reintermediation was thus needed and necessary. We can now better understand why electronic intermediaries emerged to fill the gap left by traditional channel members in order for buyers and sellers to complete online commercial transactions.

Marketing functions can be grouped into three major categories: exchange functions, logistical functions, and facilitating functions (Beckman and Davidson 1967). The exchange functions include the marketing activities related to buying and selling. Thus, these are concerned with the change in ownership or title transfer. The exchange process also requires additional tasks such as finding and seeking buyers and sellers, stimulating sales by using promotional means such as sales incentives, contests, gifts, advertising, negotiating terms of trade, establishing price, and so forth. It is clear that electronic channel members can perform these marketing tasks. In fact, it is suggested that transactional activities and the process of search and double search (Alderson 1954) in some cases could be conducted more efficiently via the Internet when compared to traditional distribution channels. For example, an electronic marketplace that regroups most or all buyers and sellers within a specific industry (e.g., Covisint) can potentially ease the double search process by providing a virtual meeting place for information exchange and potential transactions. It is assumed that searching costs and transactional costs would be lower using electronic channels than traditional ones. Using transactional cost theory, Sarkar, Butler and Steinfield (1995) provide good insights as to why that may be the case. Of course, empirical evidence is needed that will either support or refute this proposition.

The logistical functions are related to the physical distribution of the product, that is the physical work needed to bring the product from the seller to the buyer. Specifically, they deal with transportation, storage, and inventory management, among others. Except for numeric goods, Internet intermediaries cannot perform these marketing functions over the Internet. Therefore, traditional channel intermediaries are still needed to perform the logistical functions.

The costs of performing the physical supply functions (i.e., the logistical functions) are far higher than the costs needed to stimulate and obtain a sale (Tamilia 1998). In fact, the ratio has been estimated to be as high as four to one. The high costs of performing logistical work can be very expensive with small orders, such as when selling to individual consumers. The following set of marketing tasks needed to bring products to market is presented in Figure 1. The potential cost efficiencies associated with their performance using the Internet is either low or non-existent.

Finally, facilitating functions, namely standardization, financing and credit, risk bearing and market information are all sub-functions that support the first two categories of marketing functions. These tasks can also be performed over the Internet, more or less, by electronic intermediaries since they are all intangible (i.e., service driven) functions. It is further suggested that facilitating functions such as risk bearing and market information can be improved for certain transactions using the

FIGURE 1. Physical Work or the Logistical Function

- Products are ordered, billed/invoiced, handled, packaged, packed, wrapped, bundled, sorted, crated, braced
- Products are assembled, stored, warehoused, loaded, unloaded, shelved, displayed, cross-docked
- Products are shipped by air, water, rail, pipeline, containers, and intermodally
- Products are exported, imported, documented, marked, consolidated
- Products are traced, tracked, recycled, disposed
- Products are serviced, repaired, returned, installed
- Products are collected, sorted and assorted
- Products are dropped-off, picked-up
- Logistical customer service standards are set (time, availability, errors, etc.)

Internet since they are mainly based on informational exchanges. For example, the overall risk associated with inventory levels can be decreased by real time information sharing across channel members (i.e., supply chain management). However, facilitating functions such as standardization, financing and credit do not seem to hold as much efficiency improvement potential if these are performed by online intermediaries instead of traditional channel members.

CYBERMEDIARIES AND MARKETING FLOWS

In order to achieve a more dynamic view of how electronic channel members can perform marketing functions, one needs to understand that when channel members perform marketing functions, "flows" are generated. Marketing flows are defined as "a set of functions performed in sequence by channel members" (Stern, El-Ansary and Coughlan 1996, page 10). In essence, marketing flows are more dynamic than marketing functions per se since they indicate the direction and ease of movement of specific activities between intermediaries within a given distribution channel. There are at least eight marketing flows: product flow, title flow or ownership, information, negotiation, financing, risking, ordering, and payment flows (Jaffe 1969; Stern, El-Ansary and Coughlan 1996). Some flows have an important informational component and their efficiency can be improved when performed by electronic channel members over the Internet, as shown in Table 1.

More specifically, these flows are title transfer, information, negotiation, risking, ordering, invoicing, and payment. For example, intelligent agent technology that matches buyers and sellers when coupled with electronic marketplaces (e.g., Bizbots.com) may improve the efficiency of marketing flows such as ownership, information and negotiation by providing buyers and sellers means to easily discover what is offered and to negotiate (sometimes anonymously) with other market participants. In addition, ordering, invoicing and payment can potentially be performed more efficiently with electronic means (i.e., EDI, Quick Response, satellite networks, bar-coding, touch-screen computerized cash registers) by reducing information delays and eliminating paper-based documents (see Stern, El-Ansary and Coughlan 1996, chapter 9). Even if information technology can improve their efficiency, many flows may also need to be done the traditional way (i.e., a customer insists on receiving a paper invoice), such that efficiencies may be hard to pinpoint due to joint costs.

TABLE 1. Potential Efficiency Improvement of Marketing Functions and Flows When Performed by Online Intermediaries

Marketing Functions	Potential Internet Efficiency Improvement	Marketing Flows	Potential Internet Efficiency Improvement
Exchange			
Buying	Yes	Ownership	Yes
Selling	Yes	Negotiation	Yes
Pricing	Yes	Information	Yes
		Payment	Yes
Logistical			
Transport	No/Yes for numeric goods	Physical possession	No/Yes for numeric goods
Storage	No/Yes for numeric goods	Ordering	Yes
Others	No/Yes for numeric goods	Billing	Yes
Facilitating			
Standardization	No	Risking	Yes
Financing and credit	No	Financing	Yes
Risk bearing	Yes		
Market information	Yes		

The next section focuses on micro economic issues of the Internet in order to arrive at a better understanding of the economic benefits of using cybermediaries. Several types of intermediaries arise as a result of specialization of labor and division of tasks (Bowersox and Morash 1987). In retail and wholesale transactions, products or services may be exchanged, credit and financing may be offered, products may be delivered, merchandising training may be offered, and product returns may be allowed. The performance of each set of tasks will differ, depending if we are dealing with the wholesale market or the retail one (Stern, El-Ansary and Coughlan 1996).

CYBERMEDIARIES AND MICRO ECONOMIC ISSUES

Similar to any type of distribution channel, market exchanges on the Internet can occur between manufacturers, or between manufacturers and wholesalers or between wholesalers, all of the B2B type; retail transactions between business and consumers (B2C) can also be carried out. The Internet can also support many other types of market exchanges such as between consumers (C2C), between consumers and various public and nonprofit organizations (governments, academic organizations, charities, NGOs, etc.), and between the latter and businesses (Turban et al. 1999). In fact, anybody can use the Internet to obtain and exchange information, and to buy or sell products and services. Since our focus is on market exchanges in distribution channels, only B2B and B2C exchanges need to be analyzed. Moreover, since B2B are expected to be far more important than B2C transactions, we will examine more closely B2B e-marketplaces.

Different Types of Products and Services

Different types of products and services can be bought and sold using electronic intermediaries. As previously mentioned, physical products cannot be delivered via the Internet. However, the Internet can increase the delivery efficiency of numeric products. Furthermore, Internet intermediaries already can provide many services traditionally reserved to bricks-and-mortar intermediaries. Services such as travel and tourism, job placement, real estate, banking and stock trading services, publishing and information dissemination, customer and supplier data management can now all be performed by intermediaries on the Internet (Turban et al. 1999).

Of course, the same traditional channel members who view the Internet as a complementary market can also offer many such services. The Internet offers them an opportunity to do business with customers they otherwise might not be able to reach. In other words, e-commerce may offer new market segments for established sellers. By doing so, they may well need the expertise of more specialized electronic channel members to help them reach those segments. This process is very similar to a seller wanting to sell in a new market that requires the use of specialized wholesalers and retailers who distribute in that specific market.

Different Types of Cybermediaries

Internet intermediaries can participate in retail and/or wholesale exchanges. Not all online intermediaries conduct direct transactions with buyers. But they all contribute in closing the numerous market gaps that exist between sellers and buyers along the distribution chain by creating value added benefits to buyers (Mc Innes 1964).

Internet intermediaries can be classified as follows: retailers (many types according to goods and services offered), merchant wholesalers, functional middlemen or facilitating agencies (see Table 2). These functional middlemen do not take title to goods but act as a go-between buyers and sellers. They are usually paid on a commission or fee basis (i.e., brokers, agents, etc.). Although some new retailers and wholesalers have emerged with the Internet (Amazon, Expedia, etc.), the majority of the new intermediaries correspond to functional middlemen (eBay, ShopYahoo, PlasticsNet, etc.), and facilitating agencies (Altavista, Google, etc.).

Furthermore, the Internet has given rise to B2C functional middlemen that were not as visible in more traditional distribution channels. Of course, nonstore retailing has been around for a very long time. For example, Sears first started as a mail order catalogue seller back around 1875, but only opened its first store in 1925. So Sears was a B2C retailer (i.e., nonstore retailer) and the medium used for conducting business was the postal system. In other words, the U.S. Postal Service was in fact Sears' facilitating "channel" agency, similar to the role electronic intermediaries play today on behalf of many sellers on the Internet.

Since all these online intermediaries contribute to the creation of one or more economic utilities, consequently they also perform one or more marketing flows. As illustrated in Table 3, Internet intermediaries can be analyzed with respect to their contribution to marketing flows. Beckman and Davidson (1967) provide the seminal classification system of the wholesaling sector of our economy. For example, merchant wholesalers take title to goods they resell and can thus perform all or a limited number of marketing flows. Table 3 presents the example of full function merchant wholesalers that perform all marketing flows. Many retailers also perform all marketing flows. However, it is possible that some online retailers participate in only a limited number of flows. For example, they do not take physical possession of goods that are shipped

TABLE 2. B2C and B2B Online Intermediaries

B2C Intermediaries	B2B Intermediaries
Retailers	Merchant Wholesalers
Functional middlemen (mainly brokers) B2C electronic marketplaces (eBay.com) Electronic malls (shopping.yahoo.com) Aggregators (buying groups)	Functional middlemen (mainly brokers) B2B electronic marketplaces (plasticsnet.com) Aggregators (mobshop.com)
Facilitating agencies Portals Search engines Financial institutions	Facilitating agencies Portals Search engines Financial institutions

TABLE 3. Marketing Flows Performed by Online Intermediaries

Marketing Flows/ Online Intermediaries	Merchant Wholesalers (Full function)	Retailers	Functional Middlemen (Agents/Brokers)	Facilitating Agencies
Physical possession	Yes	Yes	No	No
Ownership	Yes	Yes	No	No
Information	Yes	Yes	Yes	Yes
Negotiation	Yes	Yes	Yes	No
Financing	Yes	Yes	No	No
Risking	Yes	Yes	No	No
Ordering	Yes	Yes	Yes	No
Payment	Yes	Yes	Yes/No	Yes (Financial institutions)/ No (others)

directly from wholesalers to consumers. Amazon.com is a classic example. This process is similar to what is often done in industrial markets when goods are "drop shipped" to customers in order to save logistical costs. Drop shipping is also done in consumer markets when the retail store has floor display models and the supplier is simply instructed to ship the purchased goods directly to the consumer, bypassing completely the retail store in order to save logistical costs.

Functional middlemen are specialized intermediaries limiting themselves to perform only a select number of marketing flows. They do not take titles to the goods they resell. These B2C brokers, such as online aggregators, act as a buying group for consumers interested in buying a particular product, participate in the promotion, negotiation, ordering and payment flows, but do not participate in the physical possession, ownership, financing, or risking flows. Furthermore, B2B electronic marketplace (B2B e-marketplace, hereafter) also act as brokers between buyers and sellers, since they essentially participate in the same marketing flows as the B2C aggregators. Finally, facilitating agencies such as portals (corporate or public) and search engines usually only participate in the promotion and/or informational flow, while other facilitating agencies, such as financial institutions, only participate in the payment flow.

Online brokers such as B2B e-marketplaces are anticipated to play an increasingly important role in the near future (Andrew, Blackburn and Sirkin 2000; Emiliani 2000). As a result, more is said about these relatively new online intermediaries in the next section.

B2B ELECTRONIC MARKETPLACES

According to Arndt (1979), a market can be defined as a "physical meeting place for buyers and sellers." Following this definition, e-marketplaces can be defined as a virtual meeting place for buyers and sellers as well as facilitating agents. These B2B e-marketplaces are now flourishing on the Internet. According to Andrew, Blackburn and Sirkin (2000), there are now more than 700 Internet intermediaries that can be qualified as B2B e-marketplaces in the U.S. alone. B2B e-marketplaces can either have a vertical orientation, providing services to a specific industry, or have a horizontal orientation therefore providing specific services needed by many industries (Herschlag and Zwick 2000).

At the present time, most of them only provide a limited number of services and can therefore participate in a limited number of marketing flows. It is anticipated that only a few B2B e-marketplaces within specific industries will survive. They will need to add more services if they wish to stay in business (Cap Gemini Ernst & Young 2000; Andrew, Blackburn and Sirkin 2000). Hence, some B2B e-marketplaces could evolve from functional middlemen participating in a limited number of flows, as illustrated in Table 3, to full function merchant wholesalers, involved in physical possession and ownership flows (Andrew, Blackburn and Sirkin 2000). In addition to marketing flows, some B2B e-marketplaces may even offer services that will enhance collaboration between supply chain members such as platforms for collaborative product design, sales forecasting and planning tools (Andrew, Blackburn and Sirkin 2000; Emiliani 2000).

As shown in Table 4, B2B e-marketplaces can be categorized by their ownership and membership characteristic (Sculley and Woods 1999). The classification provides a clearer understanding of why some B2B e-marketplaces may be owned by one or more channel members resulting in potential benefits for all members. Some B2B e-marketplaces can either be public or private. Public B2B e-marketplaces are open to any buyer or seller who wishes to become a member of the B2B e-marketplace. Private B2B e-marketplaces are restricted only to selected buyers and sellers that have been chosen by the B2B e-marketplace members

TABLE 4. Some B2B E-Marketplaces Grouped by Type of Ownership and Member Characteristic

Ownership/Membership	Public	Private
Channel Member(s)	Covisint Worldwide Retail Exchange	Wal-Mart GlobalNetXchange
Non Channel Member(s)	PlasticsNet Sciquest	NA

and/or owners. For example, Wal-Mart manages a private B2B e-marketplace reserved exclusively for its current list of suppliers. It should be noted that such private e-marketplaces had their start as EDI.

Moreover, B2B e-marketplaces can be owned by channel members themselves or by non-channel members. The ownership dimension is not trivial given that some buyers and sellers may be reluctant to become members of B2B e-marketplaces owned by channel members compared to B2B e-marketplaces owned by non-channel members. Examples of private B2B e-marketplaces owned by channel members include the ones operated by Wal-Mart or by Sears, Roebuck, Carrefour, Oracle, Metro AG, Sainsbury, and Kroger (GlobalNetXchange). Covisint (owned by General Motors, DaimlerChrysler, Ford Motor, Nissan and Renault) and Worldwide Retail Exchange (owned by Ahold, Albertson's, Auchan, Casino, Kmart, Target, Tesco, Safeway, CVS, Marks and Spencer, and Kingfisher) are examples of two major public B2B e-marketplaces owned by channel members (Lewis 2000). Finally, non-channel members such as industrial entrepreneurs or information technology companies own some public B2B e-marketplaces. PlasticsNet (plastics industry) and Sciquest (chemical industry) are two examples of public B2B e-marketplaces owned by non channel members (Andrew, Blackburn and Sirkin 2000; Sculley and Woods 1999).

The economics of electronic intermediaries on the Internet also have political ramifications and/or consequences. The next two sections of the paper discuss some micro and macro political issues of cybermediaries.

CYBERMEDIARIES AND MICRO POLITICAL ISSUES

In order to assess some of the micro political issues of distribution channels on the Internet, a number of discussion points are presented.

These relate to the management of power and conflict issues, as well as consequences on channel relationship and neutrality. A number of examples illustrate some of the political dimensions of using electronic intermediaries.

Managing Power and Neutrality

As previously discussed, B2B e-marketplaces can be owned by powerful channel member(s) within a given industry. Furthermore, they can restrict their access to specific channel members by operating private B2B e-marketplaces. These realities may contribute to a shift in the power structure or even enlarge the power discrepancy within specific distribution channels. Furthermore, some B2B e-marketplaces may not be attractive to some buyers and sellers because channel members own them, whether these are powerful or not. According to Sculley and Woods (1999), this ownership problem has prevented the World Insurance Network e-marketplace to become widely accepted in the insurance industry. This e-marketplace was initially owned and controlled by six insurance brokers. Insurance companies did not want to participate in a broker-owned e-marketplace.

Similarly, Sarkar, Butler and Steinfield (1995) discuss the French Teletel system, a system available to all businesses and to over 40% of consumers. Air France made use of it by permitting online seat reservation. In its bid to secure more corporate business, it planned to give to some customers a ticket printer. Even though it is a public e-marketplace, Air France had to abandon its plan for fear that traditional travel agencies would retaliate and give more business to competing airlines.

A private B2B e-marketplace owned by a single channel member might want to establish closer ties with its suppliers. Closer collaboration may lead to routinized transactions and allow the channel member to invest in more non-core business activities, such as an improved technological infrastructure among all members (Emiliani 2000). Such activities may be outsourced to specialized electronic intermediaries in order to have the various marketing flows executed more efficiently. A private B2B e-marketplace, such as an extranet instead of a public B2B e-marketplace, may provide the owner with added value benefits such as more direct ties with suppliers and customers, resulting in cost savings on membership and transaction fees. Thus, such an e-marketplace may actually spur the need for more channel members rather than less, as it may often be assumed.

Cybermediaries and the Management of Conflict

Horizontal competition, that is competition between channel members of the same type and at the same level in the channel (i.e., competing retailers), can give rise to conflict. Intertype competition, that is competition between firms operating at the same level in the channel but part of a different industry group (i.e., department store versus discount store), can also give rise to conflict. Finally, vertical conflict between channel members at different levels (vertical competition) within the same channel can also take place (i.e., wholesaler versus retailer).

The existence of horizontal and vertical competition is a business fact among electronic intermediaries as is the case among conventional channel members. Such a market reality leads to conflicting relations among the various participants. However, firms using the Internet are mostly concerned with intertype conflict that arises between competitive distribution channels. For instance, retailers typically do not consider manufacturers as competitors but as suppliers. However, the Internet gives manufacturers and wholesalers opportunities to disintermediate their distribution arrangement and to sell directly to intermediate and final buyers.

However, this disintermediation strategy may irritate and even offend traditional intermediaries and create much conflict (Alba et al. 1997). As an example of this type of conflict, Levi's initial Internet strategy was to sell directly to consumers. However, their major retail partners, such as JCPenney and Macys, suggested otherwise and told Levi to stop selling jeans via its website or suffer the consequences (Reda 1999). The previous Air France example is also applicable here. Home Depot is a more recent example. It warned all its suppliers, notably Black & Decker, that if products were sold on their websites, the company would remove their products from all company stores. Many manufacturers and franchisers are now looking at ways to integrate the Internet with traditional channels in order to achieve economies in the performance of marketing functions and flows (e.g., the car industry). A manufacturer, for instance, may enable customers to obtain competitive price information among its various dealers, to order online, and have order fulfillment performed at the regional or local dealer's or franchisee's location (Reda 1999).

CYBERMEDIARIES AND MACRO POLITICAL ISSUES

Channels of distribution are influenced by external political forces as well (Stern and Reve 1980). Many view the Internet as a bastion of free speech where curtailment of information on the Internet is an affront to democratic rights and freedom of expression. The reality is that electronic channel members, similar to conventional channels, will be subject to restrictions that will warrant government intervention in cyber-space. Eventually, trade associations, parents, teachers, and even consumers will clamor for a more restricted use of the Internet, and what electronic intermediaries can or cannot do in order to ensure fair competition and distributive justice.

With respect to fair competition, some micro-political aspects of cyber-channels may cause competitors and trade associations to ask governments (local and national) to legislate in order to ensure that all channel members are treated equitably. For example, the sales tax issue is a major concern among retailers, especially in the U.S. Bricks and mortar retailers feel they are at a disadvantage with e-tailers, given that the latter do not charge sales tax to consumers (Gleckman 2000). Local governments are also at a disadvantage, given that sales tax revenues are an important source of income for thousands of communities across the U.S. Many counties in the U.S. set their own sales tax rate for economic development purposes to attract both business and consumers. Furthermore, the misuse of the Internet by channel members, in particular B2B e-marketplaces, may generate essential facilities and collusive information exchange legal suits (see Bloom, Milne and Alder 1994 for a discussion of how information technologies can be misused in marketing).

Some B2B e-marketplaces may prohibit smaller companies from using them if they do not have the technical and financial strength to join (Andrew, Blackburn and Sirkin 2000). If cybermediaries and especially B2B e-marketplaces become major players in the distribution of certain goods and services in the economy, governments may well need to intervene. Such actions may be necessary in order to promote competitive e-marketplaces in order to avoid monopoly formation and unfair trade practices. After all, a market, whether in cyber-space or not, needs to be fair and equitable for all channel members, including consumers.

As far as Internet accessibility is concerned, it raises an important distributive justice question. What happens if only a fraction of firms within an industry has access to the Internet and electronic intermediaries? By the same token, what about those consumers who do not have access to the Internet? If the Internet (and access to cybermediaries) is not open and/or accessible to all channel members or to society in general, it may restrict consumers from enjoying some of the benefits that Internet-based transactions may offer (notably informational ones). Moreover, firms in some particular industries may not have freedom of choice to participate in some of these virtual distribution channels or e-marketplaces.

In most of the developed countries, only a portion of households has access to the Internet, according to the Ernst & Young 2000 study (e.g., Canada 39%, United States 34%, United Kingdom 29%, Australia 22%). Of course, these percentages have increased steadily since the Ernst & Young study (e.g., Canada 51% at the end of 2000). The difference is even more accentuated in developing countries. For example, in most of Latin American countries (and in Asia), less then 3% of their citizens are connected to the Internet (Marshall and Morales 1999). This problem, aptly called the "digital divide," is not only a major issue for developing countries but is also one for the poor and disadvantaged living in rich countries. No wonder the U.S. and Canadian governments have addressed the issue and have in fact started to provide incentives and subsidies for the less fortunate members of our society so they may have equal access to the Internet and gain the benefits from using it (e.g., U.S. Department of Commerce 2000).

These statistics highlight the fact that at the present time, not all consumers have access to the Internet. Even if all consumers had Internet access, it does not follow that they will all be able to make transactions due to payment or credit restrictions and sellers' unwillingness to sell in some markets. For example, numerous U.S. e-tailers simply refuse to sell to Canadian consumers due to the complications involved in distributing products across the border (exchange rates, import duties, GST, provincial sales taxes, etc.).

CONCLUSION

The main objective of this paper was to assess some economic and political issues related to the Internet as a distribution channel. The micro/macro political economy ideas provide a rich analysis of such issues.

Both micro and macro economic dimensions suggest that electronic marketing channels have the potential of improving the efficiencies related to the performance of some marketing functions and flows. Empirical research is sorely lacking to assess the extent to which the Internet can actually help reduce transaction costs and help make the marketing work more efficient. Notwithstanding the economics of e-marketplaces, micro and macro issues also need to be carefully planned and managed by channels members in order to avoid negative political reactions from other channel members, consumers, and governments as well.

This paper represents an initial effort to increase our understanding of electronic distribution channels. Many economic and political issues have been identified, but few have been analyzed in depth. Furthermore, many other social and business issues have not been discussed (e.g., privacy, security, web advertising and promotion, gambling, pornography, children, etc.). Therefore, additional theoretical and empirical work is needed in order to assess the roles and responsibilities of cybermediaries, and how they will impact conventional channels of distribution and society in general.

For sure, we need a better classification system of such electronic channel members; similar to the one developed by the Bureau of Census in the traditional retail and wholesale markets. Only then will we be better able to assess their economic contributions and their growth prospects over time.

Finally, there is an urgent need to empirically test more thoroughly the so-called "cost efficiencies" or costs savings electronic intermediaries bring to the market. All too often, it is assumed that their business model automatically provides cost savings relative to the same work done by traditional channel members. Figure 2 presents a typical list of certain business tasks.

A quick glance enables us to ask a number of questions. For example, is the cost of acquiring a new customer online less than the cost of using traditional means of distribution? Are the costs associated with introducing a new product online less than the costs of using traditional channel members? Are Internet market surveys more cost effective and reliable than those done the traditional way?

A case in point is the e-grocery business. The logistical costs would tend to preclude the use of a mass home delivery distribution system for such products. After all, grocery items are purchased weekly and with great ease at numerous locations by consumers in any given week (supermarkets are opened 24 hours a day, close proximity, wide assortment of in-store services, returnable bottles, coupons, in store specials,

FIGURE 2. Can Cybermediaries Perform These Marketing Tasks More Efficiently Than Traditional Channel Members?

• Advertising	• New product development costs
• Cost of buildings and materials	• New product introduction costs
• Cost of keeping a customer	• Packaging
• Cost to reach a customer	• Packing
• Credit costs	• Personnel selling
• Customer acquisition cost	• Product assortment
• Delivery	• Product return
• Handling customer complaints	• Purchasing
• Inventory costs	• Sales promotion
• Loyalty programs	• Small orders
• Marketing research	• Transportation

etc.). Irrespective of the tremendous costs associated with home delivery, no one has yet addressed the question of how new grocery items can be introduced using cyber-grocery channels, and at what costs, given that the supermarket industry introduces over 20,000 new items each year. Moreover, cyber-grocery channels look only at B2C exchanges when in reality, B2B ones may be even more important for the success of such cyber-channels. After all, where will these cybermediaries obtain their grocery items and what is their bargaining power with their suppliers?

It is not yet known if cybermediaries can perform the tasks listed above more efficiently than when the same tasks are carried out by traditional channel members. The answer would shed light as to the economic value and potential growth of e-tailing and other such e-marketplaces.

REFERENCES

Alba, Joseph, John Lynch, Barton Weitz, Chris Janiszewski, Richard Lutz, Alan Sawyer, and Stacy Wood (1997), "Interactive Home Shopping: Consumer, Retailer, and Manufacturer Incentives to Participate in Electronic Marketplaces," *Journal of Marketing*, Vol. 61 July, pp. 38-53.

Alderson, Wroe (1954), "Factors Governing the Development of Marketing Channels," in Richard Clewett ed. *Marketing Channels for Manufactured Products*, Richard D. Irwin, pp. 35-40.

Andrew, James, Andy Blackburn and Harold Sirkin, (2000), *The B2B Opportunity: Creating Advantage Through E-Marketplaces*, The Boston Consulting Group, October.

Arndt, Johan (1979), "Toward A Concept of Domesticated Markets," *Journal of Marketing*, Vol. 43 Fall, pp. 69-75.

Arndt, Johan (1983), "The Political Economy Paradigm Foundation for Theory Building in Marketing," *Journal of Marketing*, Vol. 47 Fall, pp. 44-54.

Bailey, Joseph and Yannis Bakos (1997), "An Exploratory Study of the Emerging Role of Electronic Intermediaries," *International Journal of Electronic Commerce*, Vol. 1 No. 3, pp. 7-20.

Beckman, Theodore and William Davidson (1967), "Nature of Functional Analysis," in *Marketing*, 8th Edition, NY: Ronald Press, pp. 417-429.

Bloom, Paul, George Milne and Robert Alder (1994), "Avoiding Misuse of New Information Technologies: Legal and Societal Considerations," *Journal of Marketing*, Vol. 58 January, pp. 98-110.

Bowersox, Donald and Edward Morash (1987), "Marketing Concept Integration and the Division of Labor," in Terence Nevitt and Stanley Hollander eds., *Marketing in Three Eras*, Proceedings of the 3rd Conference on Historical Research in Marketing, East Lansing, MI: Michigan State University, pp. 215-224.

Cap Gemini Ernst & Young (2000), "Etail IT 2000," *Chain Store Age*, Section 2, October.

Carr, Nicholas G. (2000), "Hypermediation: Commerce as Clickstream," *Harvard Business Review*, Vol. 78 January-February, pp. 46-47.

Emiliani, M. L. (2000), "Business-to-Business Online Auctions: Key Issues for Purchasing Process Improvement," *Supply Chain Management: An International Journal*, Vol. 5 No. 4, pp. 176-186.

English, Wilke (1985), "The Impact of Electronic Technology Upon the Marketing Channel," *Journal of the Academy of Marketing Science*, Vol. 13 No. 3, pp. 57-71.

Ernst & Young (2000), *Global Online Retailing*, Ernst & Young LLP, January.

Gellman, Robert (1996), "Disintermediation and the Internet," *Government Information Quarterly*, Vol. 13 Number 1, pp. 1-8.

Gleckman, Howard (2000), "The Great Internet Taxes Debate," *Business Week*, March 27, pp. 228, 230, 234, 238.

Herschlag, Miriam and Rami Zwick (2000), "Internet Auctions: Popular and Professional Literature Review," *Quarterly Journal of Electronic Commerce*, Vol. 1 No. 2, pp. 161-186.

International Data Corporation (1999), in "E-Retail, The Race Is On: Who Will Win Canada's Internet Shoppers?", *IBM Canada Ltd. and the Retail Council of Canada*.

Jaffe, Eugene D. (1969), "A Flow-Approach to the Comparative Study of Marketing Systems," in Jean Boddewyn ed., *Comparative Management and Marketing Texts and Readings*, Scott Foresman, pp. 160-170.

Keep, Lewis and Stanley Hollander (1992), "The Promise of Nonstore Retailing: A Look at the Mail Order Experience," *Journal of Marketing Channels*, Vol. 1 No. 3, pp. 61-84.

Lewis, Len (2000), "The Next Killer App," *Progressive Grocer*, Vol. 79 No. 5, May, pp. 125-130.

Libresco, Joshua (1997), "Internet commerce threatens intermediaries," *Marketing News*, Vol. 31 No. 24, November 24, page 11.

Mallen, Bruce (1973), "Functional Spin-Off: A Key to Anticipating Change in Distribution Structure," *Journal of Marketing*, Vol. 37 July, pp. 18-25.

Marshall, Dale and Ruben Morales (1999), "FTAA-Joint Government-Private Sector Committee of Experts on Electronic Commerce," *Free Trade Area of the Americas*, November 4.

Mc Innes, William (1964), "A Conceptual Approach to Marketing," in Reavis Cox, Wroe Alderson and Stanley Shapiro eds., *Theory in Marketing*, Irwin, pp. 51-67.

Palamountain, Joseph (1955), *The Politics of Distribution*, Cambridge, Harvard University Press.

Pelton, Lou, David Strutton and James Lumpkin (1997), *Marketing Channels: A Relationship Management Approach*, Irwin/McGraw-Hill.

Peterson, Robert, Sridhar Balasubramanian and Bart Bronneberg (1997), "Exploring the Implications of the Internet for Consumer Marketing," *Journal of the Academy of Marketing Science*, Vol. 25 No. 4, pp. 329-346.

Reda, Susan (1999), "Internet Channel Conflicts," *Stores*, Vol. 81 No. 12 December, pp. 24-28.

Sarkar, Mitra, Brian Butler and Charles Steinfield (1995), "Intermediaries and Cybermediaries: A Continuing Role for Mediating Players in the Electronic Marketplace," *Journal of Computer Mediated Communication*, Vol. 1 Number 3, pp. 1-14 (www.ascusc.org/jcmc/vol1/issue3/sarkar.html).

Sculley, Arthur and William Woods (1999), *B2B Exchanges: The Killer Application in the Business-to-Business Internet Revolution*, ISI Publications.

Shaw, Eric (1994), "The Utility of the Four Utilities Concept," in Jagdish Sheth and Ronald Fullerton eds., *Explorations in the History of Marketing*, Greenwich, CT: JAI Press Supplement 6, pp. 47-66.

Stern, Louis and Torger Reve, (1980), "Distribution Channels as Political Economies: A Framework for Comparative Analysis," *Journal of Marketing*, Vol. 44 Summer, pp. 52-64.

Stern, Louis, Adel El-Ansary and Anne Coughlan (1996), *Marketing Channels*, 5th Edition, Upper Saddle River, NJ: Prentice Hall.

Tamilia, Robert D. (1998), "Logistics: Toward A Managerial Revolution," in Gilles St. Amant and Mokhtar Amami eds., *Electronic Commerce: Infrastructure and Development of Management Systems*, Proceedings of the Third International Conference on the Management of Networked Enterprises, Montreal, Canada, pp. 432-461.

The Economist (2000), "Survey: E-Commerce: First America, then the World," Vol. 354 February 26, pp. S49-S53.

Turban, Efraim, Jae Lee, David King, and Michael Chung (1999), *Electronic Commerce: A Managerial Perspective*, Upper Saddle River, NJ: Prentice Hall.

U. S. Department of Commerce (2000), *Digital Economy 2000*, Washington, DC: Economics and Statistics Administration, June (www.ecommerce.gov).

A Three-Tier Model Representing the Impact of Internet Use and Other Environmental and Relationship-Specific Factors on a Sales Agent's Fear of Disintermediation Due to the Internet Medium

Rajesh Gulati
Dennis Bristow
Wenyu Dou

SUMMARY. Much has been written in both the popular and academic literatures about the impact of the Internet on the professional salesperson. However, relatively little attention has been devoted to the impact of the Internet medium on the independent sales agent as a channel intermediary. To address this issue, the current study developed and tested a conceptual

Rajesh Gulati is Assistant Professor of Marketing, Dennis Bristow is Associate Professor of Marketing and Director, Business Research Office, and Wenyu Dou is Assistant Professor of Marketing, all at the G. R. Herberger College of Business, St. Cloud State University, St. Cloud, MN 56301.

Address correspondence to Rajesh Gulati (E-mail: rgulati@stcloudstate.edu).

The authors would like to thank Mr. Joe Miller and Mr. Jerry Leth from the Manufacturer's Agents National Association for their help and support in making this research project possible.

[Haworth co-indexing entry note]: "A Three-Tier Model Representing the Impact of Internet Use and Other Environmental and Relationship-Specific Factors on a Sales Agent's Fear of Disintermediation Due to the Internet Medium." Gulati, Rajesh, Dennis Bristow, and Wenyu Dou. Co-published simultaneously in *Journal of Marketing Channels* (Best Business Books, an imprint of The Haworth Press, Inc.) Vol. 9, No. 3/4, 2002, pp. 49-85; and: *Internets, Intranets, and Extranets: New Waves in Channel Surfing* (ed: Audhesh Paswan) Best Business Books, an imprint of The Haworth Press, Inc., 2002, pp. 49-85. Single or multiple copies of this article are available for a fee from The Haworth Document Delivery Service [1-800-HAWORTH, 9:00 a.m. - 5:00 p.m. (EST). E-mail address: getinfo@haworthpressinc.com].

framework which posits relationships between nine component constructs (i.e., assortment complementarity, product/market idiosyncracy, agent's Internet utilization, relationship-specific adaptation by the manufacturer, agent's role salience, information exchange, awareness of disintermediation, perceived satisfaction, and perceived threat of disintermediation). Utilizing information gathered from a national sample of independent sales agents, the study presents the results of confirmatory factor analysis and path analysis and suggests avenues for future research. *[Article copies available for a fee from The Haworth Document Delivery Service: 1-800-HAWORTH. E-mail address: <getinfo@haworthpressinc.com> Website: <http://www. HaworthPress.com> © 2002 by The Haworth Press, Inc. All rights reserved.]*

KEYWORDS. Disintermediation, Internet utilization, independent sales agents, channel member viability, role-salience, assortment complementarity, information exchange

INTRODUCTION

It is only partial truth to say that the Internet will replace consultative salespeople. It has replaced many of them, but will never replace them all. (Canada, 2001; p. 1)

Manufacturers and distributors face the possibility of eating their own children in order to survive. We're looking at the dismantling of some existing distribution and sales channels. (e-commerce analyst Vernon Keenan in *Information Week*, 2000; p. 1)

The above excerpts from the popular press exemplify an emerging debate as to the future viability of the independent sales agent, a valuable channel of distribution in both business and reseller markets, in the Internet era. As Peterson et al. (1997) emphasize, the Internet not only provides a vast sea of information at minimal cost, but also has the potential to serve as an innovative marketing channel for various members of a channel of distribution. Indeed, some manufacturers and suppliers now conduct business directly with each other through the Internet. Such exchange relationships are becoming more common in the automobile and personal computer industries as well as in the service industries including insurance and travel. An intensification of this trend in business-to-business marketing (i.e., marketing exchanges in which a manufacturer, reseller, non-profit organization or any other institution besides the ultimate consumer may serve as the buyer) has the potential to threaten the survival of independent sales agents. Therefore, the study of possible disintermediation of independent sales agents by the Internet becomes an important area of investigation in marketing.

The fact that the Internet serves as a prodigious storehouse of information available interactively at a very low cost (Peterson et al., 1997) also suggests that channel members such as independent sales agents can utilize Internet resources to become more efficient and effective, and thus provide greater value to their principals. As a unique communication medium (Hoffman & Novak, 1996), the Internet also offers opportunities for improved communication between independent sales agents and their principals. As yet, extant research has not investigated two important questions: (1) whether and how channel members such as independent sales agents can use the Internet as an effective tool, and (2) whether and how the potential advantages derived from utilization of the Internet medium might influence the viability of the independent sales agent as a channel member.

Prior research on independent sales agents has primarily examined factors that influence a manufacturer's choice between two channel alternatives: independent sales agents and employee sales force (e.g., Anderson, 1985; Anderson & Schmittlein, 1984; Dutta et al., 1995; John & Weitz, 1988; Weiss & Anderson, 1992). Some factors that relate to such a choice include trade-offs between costs and benefits (Anderson, 1985; Anderson & Coughlan, 1987; Coughlan, 1985; Day & Klein, 1987; John & Weitz, 1988; Klein, Frazier, & Roth, 1990), and asset specificity and environmental uncertainty (e.g., John & Weitz, 1988; Klein, Frazier, & Roth, 1990; Weiss & Anderson, 1992). In the current environment, a third alternative exists: manufacturers and buyers can opt to conduct business online without utilizing independent sales agents or, alternatively, by minimizing the use of a proprietary sales force. What impact, then, does the environment in which a manufacturer operates, and any adaptation the manufacturer makes on behalf of a buyer, have on the current channel choice of the manufacturer and/or the buyer? How is the independent sales agent impacted because of the new marketing channel alternative available to a manufacturer and/or supplier? These are salient questions that remain to be addressed adequately by marketing scholars.

As the above paragraphs outline, there are several important research prerogatives concerning the investigation of the impact of the Internet on independent sales agents who comprise an indirect channel of distribution in business markets. This study develops a framework that incorporates environmental and relationship-specific factors in an attempt to answer some of the questions raised above. Specifically, this study examines the issue from the perspective of independent sales agents and attempts to answer the following research questions:

1. What relationships, if any, exist between (a) product-market related environmental factors, (b) an independent agent's role-salience in his or her relationship with a principal, and (c) the extent to which an independent sales agent perceives that he/she will be disintermediated by the Internet medium?
2. What relationship, if any, exists between a principal's relationship-specific adaptations for a buyer and the extent to which a sales agent perceives that he/she will be disintermediated by the Internet medium?
3. Does the extent to which an independent sales agent utilizes the Internet in his/her business communications with a principal relate to (a) the nature of information exchanged with that principal, and (b) the sales agent's perceived satisfaction regarding the relationship with that principal? If so, what is the nature of these relationships?
4. What is the relationship, if any, between a sales agent's satisfaction regarding the relationship with a principal, and the extent to which the sales agent perceives that he/she will be disintermediated in the future by the Internet medium?

The study utilizes empirical findings from channels literature, the nascent literature addressing the impact of the Internet medium on marketing, interviews with sales agents, and related business literature and theories to first conceptualize and then empirically test a model that depicts the relationships addressed by the stated research questions. The next section introduces the conceptual model that depicts the impact of Internet utilization and other antecedent constructs on an independent sales agent's information exchange, role-salience, satisfaction, and fear of disintermediation by the Internet medium (abbreviated as the Sales Agents ID model). The component constructs introduced in the model are delineated and the hypotheses implied in the model are developed. The subsequent section describes the procedures used to develop the survey instrument, collect the data, and analyze the procured data. The results of the study are then presented, followed by a discussion of the findings and managerial implications of the study.

CONCEPTUAL FRAMEWORK AND HYPOTHESES

The perceptual model depicting a sales agent's Internet utilization and fear of disintermediation (i.e., the Sales Agent's ID model, Figure 1) offers one plausible explanation of the impact of the Internet medium on the sales agent. As Figure 1 indicates, the Sales Agent's ID model presents a 3-tiered framework which depicts the impact of relevant environmental and relationship specific factors on a sales agent's fear of disintermediation by the Internet medium. The inclusion of these factors in the Sales Agent's ID model is based on their posited direct and indirect relationships with the dependent variable "Fear of Disintermediation by the Internet." The relationships depicted in the Sales Agent's ID model pertain to (a) a sales agent's behaviors and perceptions with regard to a spe-

FIGURE 1. A Conceptual Model Depicting the Impact of Internet Utilization, Product-Market Related Factors, and Relationship-Specific Behaviors on a Sales Agent's Role Salience, Satisfaction, and Fear of Disintermediation Due to the Internet Medium (The Sales Agent's ID Model)

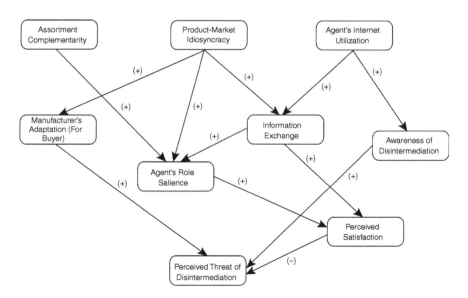

cific manufacturer the agent represents and a specific buyer of the manufacturer's products, and (b) the sales agent's evaluations of his or her relationships with that manufacturer and buyer. Those relationships are explained through the formulation of testable hypotheses.

Internet Utilization. We describe Internet utilization as the extent to which an independent sales agent uses the Internet as a medium to communicate with principals and/or with clients on behalf of the principals. Both business literature (e.g., Dos Santos & Kuzmitz, 2000; Pease, 2000) and academic treatises (e.g., Hoffman & Novak, 1996; Peterson et al., 1997) emphasize the usefulness of the Internet as a medium that enables better communication between involved parties. Weitz et al. (2001) emphasize that the Internet is a medium that enables salespeople to prospect, gather information about clients and prospects, and communicate with principals and clients. Both Peterson et al. (1997) and Hoffman and Novak (1996) underscore the utility of Internet as an innovative medium that fosters better communication.

Information Exchange. Cannon and Perreault, Jr. (1999) define information exchange as "expectations of open sharing of information that may be useful to both parties" (p. 441). Such an exchange of information includes the sharing of proprietary information, and product and market related information and is linked closely to the concept of communication (Cannon & Perreault, Jr., 1999). The above discussions on (a) the facilitating role of the Internet as a medium which improves communication between two parties, and (b) the delineation of information exchange as enhanced communication where proprietary information may be shared suggest that a sales agent who uses the Internet to communicate with his/her principal should experience greater exchange of information with principal. The Sales Agent's ID model (Figure 1) illustrates this posited relationship between Internet utilization and information exchange.

> *Hypothesis 1*: The greater the extent to which a sales agent utilizes the Internet to communicate with a principal, the greater is the information exchange between the sales agent and the principal.

Our review revealed scant literature that treats the independent sales agent as the focus of investigation. To better understand the environment in which sales agents operate, and the various roles sales agents perform, a series of discussions and consultations were undertaken with active and erstwhile sales agents. These discussions led to the conceptualization of two plausible constructs, assortment complementarity and product-market idiosyncrasy, that relate to salient value-added activities performed by independent sales agents. The two constructs are depicted in the Sales Agent's ID model (Figure 1) as exogenous factors that relate to the sales agent's role-salience and/or have an impact on the manufacturer's behaviors. For this study, we define role-salience as the importance of one channel member to the other as determined by the incremental value provided by the first channel member. A sales agent's role-salience, therefore, would refer, in part, to the extent to which a manufacturer seeks out the sales agent's advise and knowledge in the course of customizing/adapting products to match a buyer's requirements.

Assortment Complementarity. This construct describes the extent to which a sales agent represents products that complement a principal's products, and therefore, the ability of that agent to offer a more comprehensive package to a potential buyer. An independent sales agent may represent complementary products because the sales agent follows the norms that dictate the agency business, and/or the sales agent makes a voluntary effort to become a more effective channel member. In both instances, a higher degree of assortment complementarity represented by the sales agent should make that agent more valuable to the manufacturer.

Product-Market Idiosyncrasy. This construct describes the extent to which a sales agent operates in an environment where (a) the product specifications desired by a buyer vary from one purchase situation to the next and/or (b) product specifications for the same manufacturer's products vary from one buyer to another. An independent sales agent's experience with a buyer who has such idiosyncratic requirements would, in effect, make the sales agent an expert at determining the needs and requirements of that buyer. Therefore, where product-market idiosyncrasy is high, the manufacturer would tend to look to the independent sales agent to provide relevant information regarding product adaptations and changes in product specifications. Like product complementarity, product-market idiosyncrasy should also increase the importance of the sales agent to the manufacturer. In the Sales Agent's ID model (see Figure 1), these relationships are depicted as positive and direct influences these constructs have on a sales agent's role-salience.

> *Hypothesis 2*: The greater the extent to which an independent sales agent represents offerings that complement a manufacturer's products, the greater is the role-salience of that sales agent.

> *Hypothesis 3*: The more idiosyncratic are a buyer's requirements, the greater is the role-salience of the manufacturer's sales agent.

The Sales Agent's ID model (Figure 1) suggests that, in the triadic relationship between a specific manufacturer, sales agent, and buyer, product-market idiosyncrasy relates not only to an agent's role-salience, but also influences directly and positively the information exchange between the sales agent and the manufacturer. Kelly and Thibaut (1978) asserted that exchange partners come to better understand the outcomes of their behaviors by sharing information. In the context of bargaining, Clopton (1984) found that openly sharing information leads to optimal outcomes for both the bargaining parties. These findings can be aptly applied to the situation where a buyer requires idiosyncratic changes in product specifications. Both the independent sales agent and the manufacturer stand to gain by openly sharing information in such a situation. For example, the sales agent becomes more effective when he or she has relevant product-related information to share with the supplier. Open sharing of confidential information also affords the manufacturer a means to determine the product requirements of the buyer.

Hypothesis 4: The more idiosyncratic are a buyer's requirements, the greater is the information exchange between an independent sales agent and his/her principal.

Relationship-Specific Adaptations. Cannon and Perreault, Jr. (1999) define relationship-specific adaptations as "investments in adaptations to process, product, or procedures specific to the needs or capabilities of an exchange partner . . . Williamson's (1985) notion of asset specificity is also closely related to the idea of relation-specific adaptations" (pp. 443-444). We adopt this definition of relationship-specific adaptations to represent adaptations made by a manufacturer on behalf of a buyer with idiosyncratic requirements. The Sales Agents ID model (Figure 1) depicts a direct and positive relationship between product-market idiosyncrasy and a manufacturer's adaptations. Industrial products are frequently customized to the buyer's requirements and this may require investments in research, product development, and/or manufacturing technology (Cannon & Perreault, Jr., 1999). The degree to which a supplier's requirements are idiosyncratic and/or change from situation to situation, then, should influence the extent to which a manufacturer might find it necessary to adapt its processes and products.

Hypothesis 5: The greater the product-market idiosyncrasy, the greater is the relationship-specific adaptation the manufacturer makes on behalf of a buyer.

The relationship between a manufacturer and an independent sales agent is, by its very nature, asymmetric in favor of the manufacturer. For example, the manufacturer is the final arbiter of decisions regarding product specifications, product prices, production quantities, and supply quantities. More importantly, the sales agent almost always operates under temporary contracts that can be rescinded by the principal. Open exchange of proprietary and confidential information about issues such as product specifications and production processes (i.e., information exchange between a manufacturer and a sales agent), however, is likely to reduce this asymmetry. Through information exchange, the sales agent gathers vital information about the manufacturer. Because the sales agent also procures relevant information pertaining to the requirements of a buyer, the agent becomes a vital conduit between the manufacturer and the buyer. Accordingly, the Sales Agent's ID model (Figure 1) posits a direct and positive relationship between information exchange and the agent's role-salience.

Hypothesis 6: The greater the information exchange between an independent sales agent and a manufacturer, the greater is the role-salience of the sales agent.

Perceived Satisfaction. Drawing on previous conceptualizations, Geyskens et al. (1999) define channel member satisfaction as "a positive affective state resulting from the appraisal of all aspects of a firm's working relationship with another firm" (p. 224). We adopt this definition of satisfaction to represent a sales agent's satisfaction with a manufacturer. Free exchange of information that is confidential (i.e., information exchange) is posited to be a characteristic of relational exchange (Macneil, 1990). Relational exchange between two parties is positively associated with their perceived satisfaction with the exchange relationship. Also, in buyer-seller relationships, information exchange has been found to relate directly and positively to the buyer's satisfaction (Cannon & Perreault, Jr., 1999). The Sales Agents ID model (see Figure 1) predicts a similar relationship between information exchange involving a sales agent and a principal and the sales agent's perceived satisfaction with the principal.

Hypothesis 7: The greater the information exchange between an independent sales agent and his or her principal, the greater is the agent's perceived satisfaction with the principal.

Role theory has been used effectively by researchers in psychology, social psychology and organizational behavior to show that roles play an important part in social structure (Mead, 1934; Turner, 1978). According to role theory, individuals' role expectations are influenced by both their personal attributes and the contexts in which they exist. Identity theory, a sibling of role theory, further stipulates that it is not the existence of roles but their saliency that affects behavior (Burke, 1991; Thoits, 1992). Roles that are most salient to people provide the strongest meaning or purpose (Welbourne et al., 1998). The above theories, when applied to a sales agent, imply that the sales agent's role-salience in a relationship with a manufacturer should influence positively the meaning and purpose he or she attaches to the relationship.

As discussed earlier in this section, a sales agent's role-salience is based, in part, upon the sales agent's product and market-related expertise, knowledge, and information. These are valuable resources for a manufacturer (Dwyer, Schurr, & Oh, 1987; Scheer & Stern, 1992) and therefore would be expected to facilitate symmetry in the sales agent's relationship with a manufacturer (Buchannan, 1992). The enhanced meaning and purpose a sales agent attaches to his/her relationship with a manufacturer, and the increased symmetry the sales agent achieves in the relationship with the manufacturer as a result of increased role-salience, should contribute to the sales agent's perceived satisfaction with that relationship. The Sales Agent's ID model, therefore, posits a direct and positive relationship between the sales agent's role-salience and his/her satisfaction with the manufacturer.

Hypothesis 8: The greater an independent sales agent's role-salience in his/her relationship with a principal, the greater is the perceived satisfaction of the sales agent with that relationship.

Sales Agent's Satisfaction with the Exchange Relationship. In marketing channels literature, satisfaction has been considered a central construct that (a) signals the quality and stability of relations between channel members (Gaski, 1984; Weiss & Anderson, 1992), and (b) indicates future positive performance and long lasting relationships between channel members (Anderson & Narus, 1990). Dissatisfaction with channel members, on the other hand, is a strong reason for change in the channel of distribution (Stern & El Ansary, 1988). Drawing on previous findings, we posit that a sales agent who is satisfied in his/her relationship with a manufacturer would perceive that relationship to be stable and enduring. The Sales Agent's ID model (Figure 1), consequently, indicates a direct and negative relationship between a sales agent's satisfaction and his or her fear of being disintermediated by the Internet medium.

Hypothesis 9: The greater a sales agent's perceived satisfaction with a principal, the lower is the agent's fear of being disintermediated by the Internet medium.

Relationship-specific adaptations (Cannon & Perreault, Jr., 1999) create value for the buyer (Jackson, 1985), and signal a manufacturer's commitment to doing business with the buyer (Anderson & Weitz, 1992). Closer ties between a manufacturer and a buyer may render the independent sales agent, the channel intermediary, less useful. Also, by definition, relationship-specific adaptations provide a manufacturer with valuable information about the buyer's needs and requirements. This implies that, for the relationship examined here, the sales agent's expertise might no longer be as vital to the manufacturer. A sales agent, in evaluating such a situation, could be expected to perceive that the manufacturer is likely to sell to that buyer directly as the manufacturer no longer requires the services of the agent. The sales agent's perceived threat of disintermediation would understandably be heightened by the ability of the manufacturer to opt for a low cost alternative, i.e., to sell to the buyer directly using the Internet medium.

Hypothesis 10: The greater the relationship-specific adaptation a manufacturer makes on behalf of a buyer, the greater is the independent sales agent's fear of being disintermediated by the Internet medium.

The importance and viability of electronic channels has been a continuing subject of debate among retailers and commentators for over twenty years (Quelch & Takeuchi, 1981; Reynolds & Davies, 1988). The relatively recent emergence of the Internet into the popular consciousness has encouraged proponents of electronic commerce to argue that the age of direct selling has arrived (Reynolds, 1997). Popular business literature (e.g., Abrams, 1997; Alsop, 1999; Maney, 1999) has devoted significant space in the recent past to this topic, intensifying the fear that middlemen might be disintermediated by the Internet medium.

It is logical to assume that an independent sales agent whose Internet utilization is greater (as compared to an agent whose does not utilize the Internet to the same extent) would be more likely to be cognizant of media coverage on disintermediation, especially when such coverage refers to the potential use of the Internet medium as a direct selling tool for suppliers and buyers in business markets. Also, an independent sales agent who uses the Internet in his/her selling activities, compared to his/her counterparts who use the Internet to a lesser degree (or not at all), might predictably be more aware of current applications of the Internet medium to communicate with principals and prospects in his/her industry. In essence, it is likely that the sales agent's use of the Internet as a professional selling tool provides the agent with a knowledge base that leads to greater cognizance of the value added to the channel of distribution by the use of that tool. Such an increased awareness of the usefulness of the Internet as a selling tool might quite reasonably lead to a greater awareness of the potential of the Internet to displace the sales agent. The Sales Agent's ID model (Figure 1), accordingly, posits a direct and positive relationship between a sales agent's Internet utilization and his/her awareness of disintermediation by the Internet medium.

> *Hypothesis 11*: The greater is an independent sales agent's Internet utilization, the greater is that sales agent's awareness of disintermediation by the Internet medium.

The Sales Agent's ID model further posits a direct and positive relationship between an agent's awareness of disintermediation by the Internet medium and the extent to which the agent perceives the threat of being disintermediated by that communication channel. The ordered protection motivation model (Tanner et al., 1991) indicates that knowledge about severity of threat, probability of occurrence, and coping response efficacy may decide the level of fear people experience. The predictions of this model can be applied usefully to a sales agent. For example, a sales agent with a heightened awareness of the phenomenon (i.e., disintermediation of sales agents by the Internet medium) is likely to devote significant consideration to the threat of being disintermediated by the Internet medium, the high probability of its occurrence, and the lack of effective coping mechanisms. As a result, that sales agent is likely to consider the threat of being disintermediated by the Internet medium to be real and perhaps even predictable.

> *Hypothesis 12*: The greater the extent to which the sales agent is aware of the existence of disintermediation by the Internet medium, the more threatened the sales agent feels about being disintermediated by the Internet medium in the future.

In addition to testing direct relationships posited in the Sales Agent's ID model (Figure 1), we also test certain indirect relationships derived from the above stated hypotheses:

Hypothesis 13:

   a. Through their direct and positive relationships with a sales agent's role-salience, assortment complementarity, product-market idiosyncracy, and information exchange relate indirectly and positively to a sales agent's satisfaction with a manufacturer.
   b. Through their direct and positive relationships with information exchange, product-market idiosyncrasy and a sales agent's Internet utilization relate indirectly and positively to the sales agent's role-salience.
   c. Through their direct and positive relationships with information exchange, product-market idiosyncrasy and a sales agent's Internet utilization relate indirectly and positively to the sales agent's satisfaction with a manufacturer.
   d. Through their direct and positive relationships with a sales agent's satisfaction, a sales agent's role-salience, and extent of information exchange relate indirectly and negatively to the degree to which a sales agent feels threatened by future disintermediation due to the Internet medium.
   e. Through its direct and positive relationship with a manufacturer's adaptation for a supplier, product-market idiosyncrasy relates indirectly and positively to the degree to which a sales agent feels threatened by future disintermediation due to the Internet medium.
   f. Through its direct and positive relationship with a sales agent's awareness of disintermediation, the sales agent's Internet utilization relates indirectly and positively to the degree to which the sales agent feels threatened by future disintermediation due to the Internet medium.

METHOD

This study utilized data from a survey of manufacturer's representatives that belong to a national manufacturer's agents association. The survey instrument tapped the sales agents' perceptions and behaviors concerning their relationships with manufacturers and their buyers in addition to measuring the agents' opinions and perceptions regarding Internet use and related consequences.

Participants

Participants in the study were independent sales agents, randomly selected from the membership roster of a national manufacturer's agents association. A total of 1,500 surveys were distributed, with 317 useable surveys being returned for a response rate of approximately 21%. We assessed response bias using early and late respondent comparison (see Armstrong & Overton, 1979); no significant differences were found. On average, the participants had approximately 21 years of experience as a manufacturer's representative and employed 4 salespeople. Approximately 55% of the participants were college graduates and their average sales for the last fiscal year were $8.24 million. Based upon discussions with officials from the National Manufacturer's Agents Association, the sample is considered to be representative of that association's membership.

Development of Survey Instrument and Testing

The process involved in developing the survey instrument included (a) in-depth discussions with the representatives of the national manufacturer's agents association, and (b) consultations with other marketing academicians regarding the issues of interest to the researchers. An iterative process assisted the development of the set of topics the survey addressed. Subsequently, the researchers reviewed relevant channels literature and other extant research in marketing to obtain the items that tapped the constructs of interest. Construct measures that were available from literature were incorporated and/or adapted based on whether they exhibited desirable reliability and validity. The expertise and experience of the academicians and manufacturer's association representatives provided the framework from which several additional categories of survey items were developed. This process (a) led to the specification of item-sets to measure factors that were determined to be salient for the study undertaken but for which measures did not currently exist, and (b) provided the nomological net for the measures of these factors.

Item-sets that were posited to measure a sales agent's satisfaction with the manufacturer, information exchange, and the manufacturer's adaptation for the buyer were adapted from similar measures developed by Cannon and Perreault, Jr. (1999) (Cronbach Alpha = .79, .83, and .84, respectively). Additionally, two 5 item-sets were developed to represent product-market idiosyncrasy and the sales agent's role-salience respectively. A 3 item-set was developed to represent the agents' awareness of disintermediation due to the Internet medium, while another 3 item-set was generated in order to assess the degree to which agents were concerned with disintermediation due to the Internet medium. Finally, a 5 item-set was included in the survey instrument in order to measure assortment complementarity and 6 items were included in order to determine the extent to which the manufacturer's representatives used the Internet for their business communications.

Initially, then, the survey instrument included thirty-eight items designed to represent the 9 constructs included in the Sales Agent's ID model (Figure 1). All survey items were written into a 7-point Likert type format and were then reviewed by four marketing academicians with expertise in the areas of professional selling, e-commerce/Internet marketing, consumer behavior, and marketing research. The reviewers examined the survey items for face validity and potential problems in wording, phrasing, understandability, or redundancy. The review process resulted in the rewording and revision of several items. The revised items and ten demographic questions were reviewed by several manufacturers' representatives. This procedure revealed no problems with the wording or understandability of the various item-sets. For each set of scale items, respondents were instructed to indicate, as appropriate given the scale items, either (a) the extent to which their firm had engaged in the specific activities described in the relevant scale items (response category end-points ranged from (1) Not at all to (7) Very much), or (b) the degree to which they disagreed or agreed with scale items (response category end-points ranged from (1) Strongly disagree to (7) Strongly agree). Further, for each set of scale items, a sales agent was instructed to think of a major manufacturer represented by his or her firm, and a major customer to whom the agent sold that manufacturer's product(s).

Survey Administration

In an attempt to maximize response rate in the study, the researchers worked closely with the president and the director of membership of the national manufacturer's agents association. With the cooperation of those individuals, a letter was drafted which explained the nature of the research and clearly indicated the association's support of the study. The letter served as the cover page for the survey instrument and was also adapted and included in an issue of the association's monthly agency sales magazine. The magazine issue was sent to all association members approximately two weeks prior to the distribution of the survey instrument. In addition, prior to mailing the questionnaire to the participants in the study, the agency administrators sent an e-mail message to all members asking that they "watch" for an important questionnaire in their mail.

Three days after the e-mail message was posted, the researchers mailed the survey instrument (first class via the United States Post Office) to the 1,500 randomly selected manufacturer's representatives. Ten days later, the director of membership of the manufacturer's agents association sent an e-mail message to each of the 1,500 manufacturer's representatives who received the questionnaire. In that e-mail, the reps were reminded of the importance of the study and were encouraged to complete the questionnaire if they hadn't already done so and were thanked in case they had returned the completed questionnaire. Finally, the e-mail message included contact information so that, if necessary, the rep could request a second copy of the survey instrument.

MEASURE PURIFICATION AND ANALYSIS

After validating the data (i.e., ascertaining the correctness of the responses, reverse coding, etc.) a correlation matrix of the 38 items representing the 9 constructs depicted by the Sales Agent's ID model (Figure 1) was generated. Inter-item correlations were examined to assess (a) the pattern of correlations between items representing unique constructs, and (b) the pattern of correlations between items representing different constructs. Dimensionality of the constructs was then assessed using the procedure listed by Gerbing and Anderson (1988). The 38 items were subjected to principal component analysis using the Kaiser criterion (eigenvalue ≥ 1) with varimax rotation.

The resulting 11-Factor structure was examined to assess the loadings and cross-loadings of the 38 items. Six items were observed to (a) either cross-load on more than one factor (loadings > .4), and/or (b) load on a factor that could not be identified. Further those items exhibited low loadings (loading < .5) on the factor (construct) they represented. An examination of the correlation matrix indicated that those items had statistically significant correlations with items representing other constructs but weak correlations with items representing the same constructs. After examining the content of the items, it was determined that the understandability of each item was suspect, and that each was a poor representative of the associated construct. Consequently, those six items were deleted from further analysis. A second principal component analysis with the 32 remaining items yielded a 9-Factor structure with eigenvalues >1(total variance explained = 69%). The loadings of the items corresponded to the constructs they represented, suggesting that all the constructs were unidimensional.

LISREL 8.3 was subsequently used to conduct a confirmatory factor analysis to purify and assess the unidimensionality of the construct-measures (see Anderson & Gerbing, 1988; Gerbing & Anderson, 1988). For the measurement model, the following values were observed for the various fit indices: X^2 (428 N = 317) = 670.85, p = .00; RMR = .13; GFI = .89; AGFI = .86; NFI = .87; NNFI = .94; CFI = .95; and RMSEA = .039. Although the model exhibited acceptable values for a majority of fit indices (see Bentler & Bonnet, 1980; Williams & Hollahan, 1994), two items exhibited unacceptably low squared multiple correlations (.18 and .07, respectively) and low standardized loadings (.42 and .27, respectively). Anderson and Gerbing (1988) emphasize that (a) a re-specification of a converged measurement model may both be justifiable and necessary if items in any construct-measure have either been erroneously included or mis-specified, and that (b) any re-specification should be based on both statistical benchmarks and item content. After evaluating the content of the two items with unacceptable indicants, both were deleted from further analysis.

Table 1 summarizes the findings of the re-specified measurement model in which the 30 remaining items were hypothesized to represent the 9 constructs depicted in the Sales Agents ID model (Figure 1). The fit indices (see Table 1) indicated an improvement in the fit of the re-specified measurement model over the first measurement model. The statistically significant standardized loadings exhibited by the 30 items representing the 9 constructs (see Table 1) established the convergent validity of the measures (see Anderson & Gerbing, 1988). Table 2

TABLE 1. Summary of Findings for the Respecified Measurement Model

Constructs and Items	Mean	Standard Deviation	Sq. Multiple R	Std. Loadings	t-Value	p <
Assortment Complementarity						
This manufacturer's products complement other products my firm sells	5.98	1.31	0.30	0.55	8.37	.001
Along with this manufacturer's products, the buyer purchases other related products that my firm sells	5.65	1.56	0.66	0.81	11.25	.001
The products of this manufacturer are combined with other products my firm sells to the buyer	4.75	1.96	0.27	0.52	8.07	.001
Product/Market Idiosyncracy						
This manufacturer's products are adapted to the buyer's specifications	4.90	2.11	0.43	0.66	10.30	.001
The buyer purchases this manufacturer's products with no customization	3.83	3.54	0.46	0.68	10.56	.001
In general, the various buyers of this manufacturer's products differ as to required product specifications	4.80	1.94	0.25	0.50	7.79	.001
Agent's Role Saliency						
This manufacturer seeks my firm's advice when developing product specifications for the buyer	4.90	1.65	0.69	0.83	16.25	.001
This manufacturer seeks my firm's advice when customizing products to the buyer's requirements	5.11	1.67	0.64	0.80	15.46	.001
We advise the buyer during the development of product specifications for this manufacturer's products	5.35	1.54	0.35	0.59	10.71	.001
Agent's Satisfaction with Relationship						
I am satisfied with the relationship between my firm and this manufacturer	5.72	1.39	0.47	0.69	13.41	.001
My firm regrets the decision to do business with this manufacturer (R)	5.40	1.22	0.26	0.51	9.23	.001
My firm's relationship with this manufacturer is mutually beneficial	6.21	1.11	0.78	0.88	19.03	.001
My firm's relationship with this manufacturer is worthwhile	6.34	1.00	0.83	0.91	20.00	.001
Information Exchange						
We share proprietary information	5.93	1.40	0.39	0.62	11.70	.001
We share relevant customer information	6.28	1.03	0.68	0.83	17.16	.001
We share relevant product information	6.34	.866	0.79	0.89	19.17	.001
We share supply and demand related information	6.23	.987	0.55	0.74	14.74	.001

	Mean	SD				
Agent's Use of Internet in Selling Activities						
The Internet is a tool that my firm uses to communicate with our customers	4.79	1.84	0.80	0.90	19.75	.001
My firm uses the Internet to communicate with prospects	3.70	1.88	0.59	0.77	15.59	.001
My firm uses the Internet to provide follow-up service to our customers	4.09	1.89	0.76	0.87	18.86	.001
My firm uses the Internet to communicate with our principals	5.14	1.78	0.58	0.74	15.46	.001
Manufacturer's Adaptation						
This manufacturer changed its personnel	2.31	1.81	0.33	0.58	10.56	.001
This manufacturer invested in capital equipment	3.15	2.13	0.72	0.85	16.39	.001
This manufacturer altered its production process	3.11	2.03	0.79	0.89	17.32	.001
Agent's Awareness of Disintermediation						
Manufacturers decided to sell to buyers directly via the Internet	2.66	1.80	0.78	0.88	19.48	.001
Buyers purchased from manufacturers directly via the Internet	2.74	1.81	0.94	0.97	22.87	.001
Buyers initiated purchases directly via on-line reverse auctions	2.65	1.82	0.62	0.79	16.56	.001
Agent's Perceived Threat of Disintermediation						
This manufacturer will sell its products directly via the Internet	2.92	1.78	0.70	0.84	17.84	.001
The buyer will decide to do business directly via the Internet	3.30	1.82	0.92	0.96	22.21	.001
The buyer will initiate purchases directly via on-line reverse auctions	3.08	1.86	0.67	0.82	17.35	.001

Descriptive Goodness of Fit Indices:

χ^2 (21 N = 317), p = .00   608.01
RMR   0.045
GFI   0.89
AGFI   0.86
NFI   0.88
CFI   0.95
AIC   770.76
RMSEA   0.042
NNFI   0.94

presents the results of the analysis conducted to determine the discriminant validity of the 9 constructs depicted in the Sales Agent's ID model. The X^2 difference tests conducted between all possible pairs of constructs are statistically significant (overall $\alpha = .05$; critical $\alpha = .001424$; critical $\lambda^2_{(1\ d.f.;\ p\ =\ .001)} = 10.828$), implying that the different measures of the construct exhibit discriminant validity (see Anderson & Gerbing, 1988; Bagozzi & Phillips, 1982). Together, Table 1 and Table 2 indicate that the measures of the 9 constructs possess both convergent and discriminant validity, i.e., the measures exhibit construct validity (Kerlinger, 1986).

Table 3 shows (a) the purified item-sets representing the uni-dimensional constructs in the Sales Agent's ID model, and (b) the reliabilities of those item-sets. Seven of the nine measures exhibited good consistency (Cronbach α). The item-sets representing assortment complementarity and product-market idiosyncrasy had marginally acceptable reliabilities (see Nunnally, 1978). As reliable scales that measure each of those constructs were not available, the reliabilities for those constructs, as reported in Table 3, were considered reasonable. Table 4 reports the correlation matrix for the construct-measures computed by summating the item-sets representing the constructs.

This study followed the two-step structural equation modeling procedure advocated by Anderson and Gerbing (1988). After purification of the measures (described above), a covariance matrix of the summated construct measures was generated and the linear relationships posited by the Sales Agent's ID model were tested using a path-analytic technique in LISREL 8.3. The following values were observed for the various fit indices: X^2 (21 N = 317) = 56.95, p = .00; Standardized RMR = .064; GFI = .96; AGFI = .92; NFI = .86; NNFI = .84; CFI = .91; and RMSEA = .072. Although the path model exhibited a statistically significant Chi-square, i.e., X^2 (21 N = 317) = 56.95, p = .00, the other fit indices indicated acceptable fit for the theorized model.

Table 5 reports the standardized path coefficients along with their t-values and statistical significance for the various hypothesized linear relationships. Figure 2 depicts the various paths that were tested along with their standardized path coefficients. Standardized path coefficients are standardized partial regression coefficients and therefore are useful when comparing the relative influence of various constructs (see Loehlin, 1992). As Table 5 and Figure 2 indicate, the analysis provided support for the majority of the hypothesized direct and indirect relation-

TABLE 2. Assessing Discriminant Validity: Chi-Square Difference Tests

Models/Construct Pairs	Model $\times$ 2	Δ Model $\times$ 2	p
Unconstrained Measurement Model (d.f. = 369)	608.01		
Constrained Models (d.f. = 370)			
Product/Market Idiosyncracy & Assortment Complementarity	737.78	129.77	<.001
Agent's Role-Saliency & Assortment Complementarity	730.91	122.90	<.001
Agent's Role-Saliency & Product/Market Idiosyncracy	684.12	76.11	<.001
Agent's Satisfaction With Relationship & Assortment Complementarity	729.32	121.31	<.001
Agent's Satisfaction With Relationship & Product/Market Idiosyncracy	728.02	120.01	<.001
Agent's Satisfaction With Relationship & Agent's Role-Saliency	832.78	224.77	<.001
Information Exchange & Assortment Complementarity	727.08	119.07	<.001
Information Exchange & Product/Market Idiosyncracy	728.94	120.93	<.001
Information Exchange & Agent's Role-Saliency	830.48	222.47	<.001
Information Exchange & Agent's Satisfaction With Relationship	1004.97	396.96	<.001
Agent's Internet Utilization & Assortment Complementarity	737.07	129.06	<.001
Agent's Internet Utilization & Product/Market Idiosyncracy	718.91	110.90	<.001
Agent's Internet Utilization & Agent's Role-Saliency	861.56	253.55	<.001
Agent's Internet Utilization & Agent's Satisfaction With Relationship	1178.23	570.22	<.001
Agent's Internet Utilization & Information Exchange	1155.65	547.64	<.001
Manufacturer's Adaptation & Assortment Complementarity	Did Not Converge		
Manufacturer's Adaptation & Product/Market Idiosyncracy	715.23	107.22	<.001
Manufacturer's Adaptation & Agent's Role-Saliency	891.07	283.06	<.001
Manufacturer's Adaptation & Agent's Satisfaction With Relationship	Did Not Converge		
Manufacturer's Adaptation & Information Exchange	966.16	358.15	<.001
Manufacturer's Adaptation & Agent's Internet Utilization	946.73	338.72	<.001
Agent's Awareness of Disintermediation & Assortment Complementarity	737.73	129.72	<.001
Agent's Awareness of Disintermediation & Product/Market Idiosyncracy	729.16	121.15	<.001
Agent's Awareness of Disintermediation & Agent's Role-Saliency	891.41	283.40	<.001
Agent's Awareness of Disintermediation & Agent's Satisfaction With Relationship	1181.45	573.44	<.001
Agent's Awareness of Disintermediation & Information Exchange	1271.50	663.49	<.001
Agent's Awareness of Disintermediation & Agent's Internet Utilization	963.81	355.80	<.001
Agent's Perceived Threat of Disintermediation & Assortment Complementarity	738.56	130.55	<.001
Agent's Perceived Threat of Disintermediation & Product/Market Idiosyncracy	729.94	121.93	<.001
Agent's Perceived Threat of Disintermediation & Agent's Role Saliency	892.09	284.08	<.001
Agent's Perceived Threat of Disintermediation & Agent's Satisfaction With Relationship	1178.20	570.19	<.001
Agent's Perceived Threat of Disintermediation & Information Exchange	1184.06	576.05	<.001
Agent's Perceived Threat of Disintermediation & Agent's Internet Utilization	1236.28	628.27	<.001
Agent's Perceived Threat of Disintermediation & Manufacturer's Adaptation	958.64	350.63	<.001
Agent's Perceived Threat of Disintermediation & Agent's Awareness of Disintermediation	1071.30	463.29	<.001

Note: Critical α = .001424; Critical $X^2_{(1\,d.f.,\,p=.001)}$ = 10.828; $p.$ = significance level.

TABLE 3. Reduced Scale Items and Reliabilities

Scale Items	Cronbach's Alpha
Assortment Complementarity* This manufacturer's products complement other products my firm sells Along with this manufacturer's products, the buyer purchases other related products that my firm sells The products of this manufacturer are combined with other products my firm sells to the buyer	∝ = .633
Product/Market Idiosyncracy* This manufacturer's products are adapted to the buyer's specifications The buyer purchases this manufacturer's products with no customization In general, the various buyers of this manufacturer's products differ as to required product specifications	∝ = .640
Agent's Role Saliency* This manufacturer seeks my firm's advice when developing product specifications for the buyer This manufacturer seeks my firm's advice when customizing products to the buyer's requirements We advise the buyer during the development of product specifications for this manufacturer's products	∝ = .779
Agents' Satisfaction with Relationship* I am satisfied with the relationship between my firm and this manufacturer My firm regrets the decision to do business with this manufacturer (R) My firm's relationship with this manufacturer is mutually beneficial My firm's relationship with this manufacturer is worthwhile	∝ = .826
Information Exchange (In my firm's relationship with this manufacturer it is expected that:)* We share proprietary information We share relevant customer information We share relevant product information We share supply and demand related information	∝ = .831
Agent's Use of the Internet in Sales Activities* The Internet is a tool that my firm uses to communicate with our customers My firm uses the Internet to communicate with prospects My firm uses the Internet to provide follow-up service to our customers My firm uses the Internet to communicate with our principals	∝ = .892
Manufacturer's Adaptations (Just for This Buyer:)* This manufacturer changed its personnel This manufacturer invested in capital equipment This manufacturer altered its production process	∝ = .810
Agent's Awareness of Disintermediation (In my firm's industry, manufacturer's reps have lost business in the past because:) Manufacturers decided to sell to buyers directly via the Internet Buyers purchased from manufacturers directly via the Internet Buyers initiated purchases directly via on-line reverse auctions	∝ = .908
Agent's Perceived Threat of Disintermediation (In the future my firm is likely to lose business because:) This manufacturer will sell its products directly via the Internet The buyer will decide to do business directly via the Internet The buyer will initiate purchases directly via on-line reverse auctions	∝ = .903

*For these scales, respondents were asked to think of one major manufacturer that his/her firm represented and one major customer to whom he/she sold that manufacturer's products

TABLE 3 (continued)

Reduced Scale Items and Reliabilities

Note 1: When responding to scale items pertaining to the Assortment Complementarity, Product/Market Idiosyncracy, Agent's Role Saliency, Agent's Satisfaction with the Relationship, Information Exchange, Agent's Awareness of Disintermediation, and Agent's Perceived Threat of Disintermediation constructs, participants were provided with the following response instructions: Use the following scale to indicate your degree of disagreement or agreement with each of the statements below. Circle the number that best represents your response. If you strongly disagree with a statement, circle the number "1" on the scale; if you strongly agree with the statement, circle the number "7" on the scale. Use the intervening numbers to represent intermediate levels of disagreement or agreement.

Note 2: When responding to scale items pertaining to the Agent's Use of the Internet in Sales Activities and Manufacturer's Adaptation for the Buyer constructs, participants responded using a 7-point Likert type scale with endpoint labels ranging from "1," not at to "7" very much. Participants were provided with the following response instructions: For the following statements, please indicate the extent to which your firm has engaged in the following activities.

TABLE 4. Correlation Matrix of Constructs Included in the Sales Agent's ID Model

	Construct								
	AC	PMI	ARS	ASWR	IEM	IUSA	MA	AAD	ATD
AC	1.00								
PMI	−0.04	1.00							
ARS	0.17**	0.40**	1.00						
ASWR	0.19**	0.11	0.36**	1.00					
IEM	0.19**	0.06	0.38**	0.44**	1.00				
IUSA	0.06	0.19**	0.27**	0.01	0.19**	1.00			
MA	−0.13*	0.22**	0.03	−0.02	0.04	0.22**	1.00		
AAD	−0.04	0.10	0.06	−0.11	−0.02	0.22**	0.11	1.00	
ATD	−0.02	0.03	0.03	−0.02	0.04	0.11*	0.15**	0.53**	1.00

Note 1: (*) implies correlation is significant at the .05 level (2-tailed); (**) implies correlation is significant at the .01 level (2-tailed)

Note 2: AC = Complementarity of Product Line Represented, PMI = Product/Market Idiosyncracy, ARS = Agent's Role Salience, ASWR = Agent's Satisfaction With Manufacturer, IEM = Information Exchange With Manufacturer, IUSA = Internet Use in Communication with Manufacturer, MA = Manufacturer's Relationship-Specific Adaptation on Behalf of Buyer, AAD = Agent's Awareness of Disintermediation due to the Internet Medium, ATD = Agent's Perceived Threat of Disintermediation due to the Internet Medium

ships. However, all relationships, direct or indirect, that included a path between (a) product-market idiosyncrasy and information exchange, and/or (b) satisfaction with the manufacturer and perceived threat of disintermediation due to the Internet medium were not supported by the analysis.

TABLE 5. Path Model Estimation Results

Direct Relationships		Std. Path Coeff.	T-Value	2-tailed Sig. p <
Assortment Complementarity				
Assortment Complementarity → Agent's Role Salience	γ12	.13	2.66	.01
Product/Market Idiosyncracy				
Product/Market Idiosyncracy → Manufacturer's Adaptation	γ21	.22	3.91	.002
Product/Market Idiosyncracy → Agent's Role Salience	γ22	.39	8.15	.002
Product/Market Idiosyncracy → Information Exchange	γ32	(.02)	(0.35)	n.s.
Agent's Internet Utilization				
Agent's Internet Utilization → Information Exchange	γ33	.19	3.32	.002
Agent's Internet Utilization → Awareness of Disintermediation	γ43	.22	4.00	.002
Manufacturer's Adaptation				
Manufacturer's Adaptation → Perceived Threat of Disintermediation	β61	.10	2.02	.05
Agent's Role Salience				
Agent's Role Salience → Perceived Satisfaction	β52	.23	4.26	.002
Information Exchange				
Information Exchange → Agent's Role Salience	β23	.34	7.14	.002
Information Exchange → Perceived Satisfaction	β53	.35	6.59	.002
Awareness of Disintermediation				
Awareness of Disintermediation → Perceived Threat of Disintermediation	β64	.53	11.07	.002
Perceived Satisfaction				
Perceived Satisfaction → Perceived Threat of Disintermediation	β65	(.04)	(0.89)	n.s.

Indirect Relationships	Std. Path Coefficient	T-value	2-tailed Sig. p <
Assortment Complementarity			
Assortment Complementarity → Agent's Role Salience → Perceived Satisfaction	.03	2.26	.05
Product/Market Idiosyncracy			
Product/Market Idiosyncracy → Manufacturer's Adaptation → Perceived Threat of Disintermediation	.02	2.00	.05
Product/Market Idiosyncracy → Agent's Role Salience → Perceived Satisfaction	.09	2.88	.02
Product/Market Idiosyncracy → Information Exchange → Agent's Role Salience	.007	0.35	n.s.
Product/Market Idiosyncracy → Information Exchange → Perceived Satisfaction	.007	0.35	n.s.
Agent's Internet Utilization			
Agent's Internet Utilization → Information Exchange → Agent's Role Salience	.12	3.85	.002
Agent's Internet Utilization → Awareness of Disintermediation → Perceived Threat of Disintermediation	.06	3.01	.01
Agent's Internet Utilization → Information Exchange → Perceived Satisfaction	.07	3.09	.01
Agent's Role Salience			
Agent's Role Salience → Perceived Satisfaction → Perceived Threat of Disintermediation	.009	0.87	n.s.
Information Exchange			
Information Exchange → Perceived Satisfaction → Perceived Threat of Disintermediation	.01	0.88	n.s.
Information Exchange → Agent's Role Salience → Perceived Satisfaction	.08	3.67	.002

FIGURE 2. Path Diagram Depicting Standardized Path Coefficients in the Sales Agent's ID Model

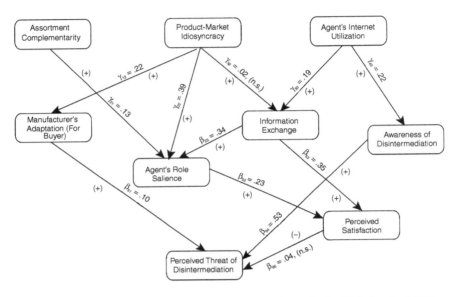

Note: n.s. implies a path that is not statistically significant; all other paths are significant in the hypothesized direction (p < .05).

A second path analysis was conducted to ascertain the fit of a revised conceptual model (Figure 3) in which the two statistically insignificant paths were deleted. The analysis yielded the following fit indices: X^2 (23 N = 317) = 57.85, p = .00; Standardized RMR = .063; GFI = .96; AGFI = .93; NFI = .86; NNFI = .86; CFI = .91; and RMSEA = .068, indicating a slightly better fit for this model. There was no discernable difference in the values of the standardized path coefficients in relation to the first path analysis. The next section discusses the results of, and implications that flow from, this study in some detail.

DISCUSSION AND IMPLICATIONS

The path-analytic model (see Figure 2) tested the effects of the 3 exogenous and 6 endogenous constructs depicted in the Sales Agent's ID model (Figure 1). Internet utilization related positively and signifi-

FIGURE 3. Respecified Sales Agent's ID Model (Insignificant Paths Deleted from the Conceptual Model)

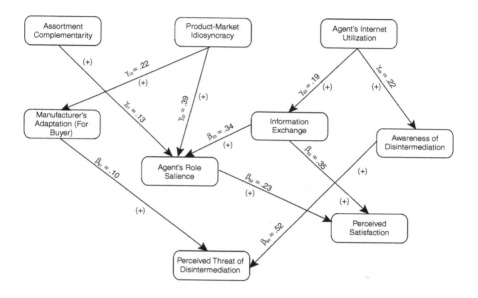

cantly ($\gamma_{33} = .19$, t = 3.32, p < .002) to information exchange, supporting Hypothesis 1. The results indicate that, for sales agents who participated in this study, utilization of the Internet medium to communicate with and on behalf of a manufacturer related directly and positively to the degree to which they exchanged vital business related information in an open manner. A generalization of this result would suggest that by increasing their utilization of the Internet as a communication medium, sales agents could improve the degree and nature of interactions with their principals.

A positive and statistically significant path ($\gamma_{21} = .13$, t = 2.66, p < .01) between assortment complementarity and role-salience suggested support for Hypothesis 2 (see Figure 2 and Table 5). For the sampled sales agents, then, the extent to which these intermediaries represent products that complement their principals' product lines relates directly and positively to how important these agents are to their principals. Generalized across all sales agents, this result indicates that sales agents who decide to enhance the assortment of complementary products for their principals are likely to become more relevant and important for the manufacturer.

The path analysis also supported Hypothesis 3, which posited a direct and positive relationship between product-market idiosyncrasy and role-salience ($\gamma_{22} = .39$, t = 8.15, p < .002; see Figure 2 and Table 5). This result establishes that sales agents who responded to the survey experience an increase in their importance to the manufacturers they represent if buyers have unique requirements that are situation-specific. These agents perceive that manufacturers need them to a greater extent to determine product specifications and obtain other related information. A generalization of this finding to all sales agents suggests that sales agents who supply buyers with idiosyncratic needs may become more important and relevant to the manufacturers they represent.

The statistically significant standardized path coefficients leading from two exogenous constructs, i.e., product-market idiosyncrasy and assortment complementarity to an agent's role-salience (see Figure 2 and Table 5) indicate that the extent to which a supplier's demands are idiosyncratic ($\gamma_{22} = .39$) relates more strongly to the agent's role-salience than does the extent to which a sales agent represents products that are complementary to the manufacturer's product line ($\gamma_{21} = .13$) (see Loehlin, 1992). In terms of influence, it can be stated that product-market idiosyncrasy exerts a greater influence on a sales agent's role-salience than the complementarity of the assortment the sales agent represents. Together these constructs explain 16.9% of the variance in an agent's role-salience (see Loehlin, 1992).

Hypothesis 4, which declares that product-market idiosyncrasy relates directly and positively to information exchange is not supported as depicted by the statistically insignificant standardized path coefficient representing this relationship ($\gamma_{32} = .02$, t = .35, p > .05; see Figure 2 and Table 5). Although the path coefficient for this relationship has the desired direction (i.e., is positive), its non-significance is unexpected in light of previous findings that seem to indicate support of this hypothesis (e.g., Clopton, 1984; Kelly & Thibaut, 1978). This result implies that for the participants in the study, increases in the degree of idiosyncratic requirements by the buyers does not relate to any increase in the openness and level of interaction between the manufacturers and their agents. A discussion of the results for Hypothesis 5, undertaken below, provides a plausible justification for this result.

A statistically significant and positive standardized path coefficient representing the direct relationship between product-market idiosyncrasy and manufacturer's relationship-specific adaptation for the buyer ($\gamma_{12} = .22$, t = 3.91, p < .002) establishes support for Hypothesis 5. This suggests that manufacturers (that responding sales agents considered when completing the survey instrument) invest in relationship-specific adaptations on behalf of buyers who have idiosyncratic requirements. The greater was the idiosyncratic nature of the requirements of buyers, the greater was the degree to which the manufacturers adapted their processes and products. An argument can be made that these manufacturers develop closer ties with the buyers as a result of these relationship-specific adaptations, a contention that has some support in marketing literature (e.g., Cannon & Perreault, Jr., 1999). A consequence of such adaptations, and the corresponding closer ties with and information about the buyers, could be that the manufacturers no longer need to discuss product/process related information with their sales agents concerning those buyers. This would explain the lack of support for Hypothesis 4 in this study.

Information exchange and role-salience related positively and significantly ($\beta_{23} = .34$, t = 7.14, p < .002), thereby supporting Hypothesis 6 (see Figure 2 and Table 5). The statistically significant path coefficient representing this relationship indicates that for sales agents who responded to the survey, there exists a direct relationship between the extent to which the agents experience high levels of interaction with the manufacturers they represent and their perceived importance to the manufacturers. A generalization of this result suggests that sales agents who encourage and/or achieve a high level of interaction with the manufacturers are likely to gain vital information and knowledge about the manufacturers' products and processes. This should enable the sales agents to better represent the manufacturers' interests and therefore make the agent more important to the manufacturers they represent.

Hypothesis 7 states that information exchange and perceived satisfaction relate directly and positively. A positive and statistically significant path coefficient ($\beta_{53} = .35$, t = 6.59, p < .002; see Figure 2 and Table 5) supports the relationship the Sales Agent's ID model posits. This result signifies that participating sales agents that experience higher levels of interactions with the manufacturers they represent are more satisfied in their relationship with their principals. One of the factors affecting an agent's satisfaction with his or her principal, therefore, is likely to be the extent to which the agent and manufacturer are open to sharing proprietary information with one another.

As predicted by the Sales Agent's ID model (Figure 1), the analysis found support for a direct and positive relationship between role-salience and perceived satisfaction ($\beta_{52} = .23$, t = 4.26, p < .002), thus Hypothesis 8 was supported. For the sampled sales agents, then, there exists a direct relationship between the extent to which they exchange proprietary and other important information with the manufacturers they represent, and the degree to which they feel satisfied in their relationships with their manufacturers. This finding supports the suggestions that flow from role and identity theories (Burke, 1991; Thoits, 1992; Welbourne et al., 1998) regarding the impact of role-salience on behavior, meaning, and purpose in relationships.

A comparison of the relationship between (a) information exchange and perceived satisfaction ($\beta_{53} = .35$), and (b) the agent's role-salience and perceived satisfaction ($\beta_{52} = .23$) indicates that the former has a stronger association with an agent's perceived satisfaction. One conclusion that derives from these associations is that a sales agent's exchange of proprietary information (higher level of interaction) with a manufacturer influences the sales agent's perceived satisfaction with the manufacturer to a greater extent than does his or her perception concerning the importance of his role to that manufacturer.

The analysis did not support the posited direct and negative relationship between a sales agent's perceived satisfaction and perceived threat of disintermediation due to the Internet medium ($\beta_{65} = .04$, t = .89, p > .05). For sales agents who responded to the survey, then, there is no relationship between how satisfied they are with their principals and the extent to which they fear that they might be disintermediated due to the Internet medium in the future. Generalized to the population of sales agents, this result implies that sales agents may be satisfied with their manufacturers and still feel the threat of disintermediation due to the Internet medium.

This finding, at first blush, is surprising because prior channels literature suggests a negative relationship between the two constructs (e.g., Anderson & Narus, 1990; Gaski, 1984; Stern & El Ansary, 1988; Weiss & Anderson, 1992). A plausible explanation for the nonexistence of this relationship in this study resides in the characteristics of the Internet medium as a marketing channel. As noted in the introduction to this study, prior research on independent sales agents has primarily examined factors that influence a manufacturer's choice between two channel alternatives–independent sales agents and employee sales force. The Internet medium presents a unique and innovative low cost communication channel (Peterson et al., 1997). To the extent that manufacturers and buyers are able to communicate with each other directly and comprehensively, the utility of the sales agent is likely to be reduced. Further, to the extent that manufacturers (and buyers) feel that conducting business through the medium of the Internet rather than using sales agents involves relatively low switching costs (Weiss & Anderson, 1992), they may be motivated to adopt the medium perceived to be more efficient. Sales agents who are satisfied with the current relationship they have with the manufacturers they represent, may therefore, still consider the Internet medium a threat to their future viability.

The results of the analysis suggest support for Hypothesis 10, which posits a direct and positive relationship between a manufacturer's relationship-specific adaptation and a sales agent's perceived threat of disintermediation due to the Internet medium (β_{61} = .10, t = 2.02, p < .05; see Figure 2 and Table 5). This result signifies that among the sales agents who participated in this study, perceptions of the extent to which manufacturers have made relationship-specific adaptations for buyers associate significantly with the degree to which these agents feel that they will be disintermediated due to the Internet medium in the future. A generalization of this finding suggests that sales agents feel more threatened that they will be disintermediated due to the Internet medium in the future if manufacturers make relationship-specific adaptations on behalf of buyers.

Hypothesis 11 relates a sales agent's Internet utilization and awareness of disintermediation directly and positively (γ_{43} = .22, t = 4.00, p < .002), and Hypothesis 12 posits a direct and positive relationship between a sales agent's awareness of disintermediation and his or her felt threat of disintermediation due to the Internet medium (β_{64} = .53, t = 11.07, p < .002). The analysis found support for both these hypotheses (see Figure 2 and Table 5). The sampled sales agents who utilized the Internet for communication with and for the manufacturers they represented were more aware of the phenomenon of disintermediation of sales agents due to the Internet medium. Further, among the sales agents who responded to the survey, an increased awareness of the existence of disintermediation due to the Internet medium was related significantly to an increased feeling that they could be disintermediated by the Internet medium in the future. These findings, when generalized across the population of sales agents, suggests that Internet utilization makes the sales agents more aware of a deleterious consequence the Internet medium may have for them and that this awareness heightens their fear of losing their business because of the Internet medium.

Of the two constructs that relate directly and significantly to a sales agent's perceived threat of being disintermediated due to the Internet medium, the agent's awareness of disintermediation ($\beta_{64} = .53$) has a greater influence than the perceived relationship-specific investments made by a manufacturer on behalf of a buyer ($\beta_{61} = .10$). Awareness of disintermediation of sales agents due to the Internet medium, therefore, seems to have a pronounced influence on a sales agents fear that he or she will be disintermediated in the future due to the Internet medium. The two factors, taken together, explain more than 29% of the variance in the dependent construct.

Table 5 also indicates statistical support for a majority of the indirect relationships that derive from the direct hypotheses the Sales Agent's ID model posits. Product-market idiosyncrasy, for example, relates indirectly and positively to (a) an agent's perceived satisfaction with the manufacturer through its direct and positive relationship with the extent to which the sales agent is important to the manufacturer (t = 2.88, p < .02), and (b) an agent's perceived fear of being disintermediated due to the Internet medium in the future through its direct and positive relationship with the extent to which a manufacturer invests in relationship-specific investments on behalf of a buyer (t = 2.00, p < .05). A sales agent's utilization of Internet for communications with and on behalf of the manufacturer relates positively and indirectly to (a) the agent's perceived satisfaction with the manufacturer through its direct and positive relationship with the extent to which he or she establishes enhanced exchange of information with the manufacturer (t = 3.09, p < .01), and (b) the agent's perceived fear of being disintermediated due to the Internet medium in the future through its direct and positive relationship with the extent to which the sales agent is aware that sales agents are being disintermediated due to the Internet medium (t = 3.85, p < .002). Table 5 further indicates that a sales agent's Internet utilization relates indirectly and positively to the sales agent's role-salience through its direct and positive relationship with the extent of information exchange with the manufacturer (t = 3.01, p < .01). These indirect relationships, coupled with the other relationships the study supports, provide some intriguing insights concerning the on-going debate surrounding the impact of the Internet on the independent sales agent as a channel intermediary.

As intermediaries between manufacturers and buyers, sales agents may face a multi-faceted entity in the Internet medium. On the one hand, the Internet provides a sales agent with an effective communication tool that can increase the level of value the agent brings to the exchange relationship. Further, the resultant increase in information exchange between the sales agent and the manufacturer tends to lead to an increase in the sales agent's role-salience and satisfaction with the exchange relationship. On the other hand, the study revealed that sales agents who utilize the Internet for their business communication had a greater awareness of instances where the Internet had in fact disintermediated the manufacturer-sales agent-buyer channel of distribution. Not surprisingly, those same sales agents perceived the Internet as a real and viable threat to their position as channel intermediaries. The Internet, therefore, seems to have both positive and negative influences for the sales agent (see Figure 4a). So the debate continues: is the Internet the sales agent's friend or foe? Is the Internet a tool the agent can use to become a more effective channel intermediary? Or is the Internet the force that will replace the agent as a channel intermediary?

The relationships between the idiosyncratic nature of the product-market in which the sales agent operates and the other constructs the study evaluated adds yet another level of complexity to the friend or foe question posed above. As noted earlier, our results showed that the higher was the degree of product-market idiosyncracy, the greater was

FIGURE 4. Depiction of Salient Indirect Relationships in the Sales Agent's ID Model

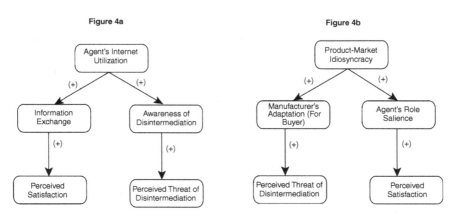

the sales agent's role-salience and satisfaction with the exchange relationship with the manufacturer. The results also showed that product-market idiosyncracy was directly and positively related to the manufacturer's relationship-specific adaptation for a buyer which, in turn, was directly and positively related to the agent's perceived threat of disintermediation (see Figure 4b). Once again, the results would seem to indicate that elements of the exchange relationship that contribute to the importance of the sales agent to the channel of distribution are linked to that agent's concern with disintermediation due to the Internet medium.

LIMITATIONS AND FUTURE RESEARCH

As this study utilized cross-sectional data to test proposed relationships, any conclusions regarding causal linkages between the constructs examined should be made with caution. Also, data was generated through self-reports, and therefore, may be biased to an extent. More significantly, the study utilized a list of sales agents belonging to one national manufacturer agents' association. Although selection of the random sample adds to its generalizability, the results of the study cannot be safely generalized to the entire population of independent sales agents. Another limitation derives from the fact that some of the constructs in the Sales Agent's ID model have been conceptualized specifically for this study and, therefore, do not have previously validated measures. This study also restricted itself to examining perceptions of sales agents, consequently the conceptual model does not evaluate the issue of disintermediation due to the Internet medium through the perspective of either manufacturers or buyers.

While our research provides some insights to the research questions posed in the study, additional research in the area is warranted. This study represents an initial empirical investigation of the Sales Agent's ID model. Several of the constructs presented in the model and the relationships posited have not been, to our knowledge, previously tested in the marketing channels literature. Researchers are encouraged to further investigate the constructs and relationships reported in this manuscript. For example, constructs conceptualized for this study should be further explicated and validated, and the issue of disintermediation of channel intermediaries due to the Internet medium should be examined from the perspectives of manufacturers and the buyers. Further understanding of the impact of the Internet on current channels of distribution should have profound influence on how, when, and where channel members devote their energies, resources, and the types of sales forces, if any, that are employed.

In addition, we encourage researchers to replicate and extend the findings reported in this manuscript. Specifically, the participant sample used in the study consisted of manufacturer's agents who belonged to a national association. While the participants did represent over 100 different industries, they constitute a rather specialized type of professional salesperson and a select type of channel structure. Accordingly, researchers are strongly urged to test the Sales Agent's ID model on a more diversified sample of sales professionals and an assortment of channels of distribution.

Yet another avenue for future research would involve investigating a diametric viewpoint, i.e., the issue of reintermediation. Given the limited financial success of many Internet-based marketing endeavors, it is plausible that under certain situations the Internet may influence reintermediation in channels of distribution. Perhaps, as marketers learn more about the contribution (or lack thereof) of the Internet to marketing exchanges, the value of channel intermediaries will be "rediscovered."

REFERENCES

Abrams, A. (1997). The threat of the net: Electronic catalogs pose challenges for forwarders, other middlemen. *Journal of Commerce and Commercial, 411* (March 31), s11.

Alsop, S. (1999). Is there an Amazon.com for every industry? *Fortune, 139* (1), 159.

Anderson, E. (1985). The salesperson as outside agent or employee: A transaction cost analysis. *Marketing Science, 4* (Summer), 234-254.

Anderson, E., & Coughlan, A. T. (1987). International market entry and expansion via independent or integrated channels of distribution. *Journal of Marketing, 51* (January), 71-82.

Anderson, E., & Narus, J. A. (1990). A model of distributor firm and manufacturing firm working partnerships. *Journal of Marketing, 54* (January), 42-58.

Anderson E., & Schmittlein, D. (1984). Integration of the sales force: An empirical examination. *Rand Journal of Economics, 15* (Autumn), 385-395.

Anderson E., & Weitz, B. (1992). The use of pledges to build and sustain commitment in distribution channels. *Journal of Marketing, 51* (January), 18-34.

Anderson, J. C., & Gerbing, D. W. (1988). Structural equation modeling in practice: A review and recommended two-step approach. *Psychological Bulletin, 103* (3), 411-423.

Armstrong, S. J., & Overton, T. S. (1977). Estimating non-response bias in mail surveys. *Journal of Marketing Research, 14* (August), 396-402.

Bagozzi, R. P., & Phillips, L. W. (1982). Representing and testing organizational theories: A holistic construal. *Administrative Science Quarterly, 27,* 459-489.

Bentler, P. M., & Bonnet, D. G. (1980). Significance tests and goodness of fit in the analysis of covariance structures. *Psychological Bulletin, 88,* 588-606.

Buchannan, L. (1992). Vertical trade relationships: The role of dependence and symmetry in attaining organizational goals. *Journal of Marketing Research, 29* (February), 65-75.

Burke, P. J. (1991). *Identity process and social stress.* American Sociological Review, 56, 836-849.

Canada, D. (2000), Web-based selling is taking a toll on sales teams. *Indianapolis Business Journal, 21*(33), 35.

Cannon, J. P., & Perreault, Jr., W. D. (1999). Buyer-seller relationships in business markets. *Journal of Marketing Research, 36* (November), 439-460.

Clopton, S. W. (1984). Seller and buying firm factors affecting industrial buyers' negotiation behavior and outcomes. *Journal of Marketing Research, 21* (February), 39-53.

Coughlan, A. T. (1985). Competition and cooperation in marketing channel choice: Theory and application. *Marketing Science, 4* (Spring), 110-129.

Day, G. S., & Klein, S. (1987). Cooperative behavior in vertical markets: The influence of transaction costs and competitive strategies. In M. Houston (Ed), *Review of Marketing* (pp. 39-66). Chicago: American Marketing Association.

Dos Santos, B. L., & Kuzmits, F. E. (1997). The Internet: A key tool for today's human resource professional. *SAM Advanced Management Journal, 62* (2), 33-40.

Dutta, S., Bergen, M., Heidi, J. B., & John G. (1995). Understanding dual distribution: The case of reps and house accounts. *Journal of Law, Economics, and Organization, 11* (1), 189-204.

Dwyer, F. R., Paul H. S., and Oh, S. (1987). Developing buyer-seller relationships. *Journal of Marketing, 51* (April), 11-28.

Gaski, J. F. (1984). The theory of power and conflict in channels of distribution. *Journal of Marketing, 48* (Summer), 9-29.

Gerbing, D. W., and Anderson, J. C. (1988). An updated paradigm for scale development incorporating unidimensionality and its assessment. *Journal of Marketing Research, 25* (May), 186-192.

Geyskens, I., Steenkamp, Jan-Benedict E. M., and Kumar, N. (1999). A meta-analysis of satisfaction in marketing channel relationships. *Journal of Marketing Research, 36* (May), 223-238.

Gilbert, A. and Bacheldor, B. (2000). The big squeeze–In suppliers' rush to sell directly to consumers over the web, sales agents, distributors, and other channel partners sorry that they'll be pushed out of the picture. *Information Week*, (March 27), 46.

Hoffman, D. L., & Novak, T. P. (1996). Marketing in hypermedia computer-mediated environments: Conceptual foundations. *Journal of Marketing, 60* (3), 50-69.

Jackson, B. B. (1985). *Winning and keeping industrial customers: The dynamics of customer relationships.* Lexington, MA: Lexington Books.

John, G., & Weitz, B. A. (1988). Forward integration into distribution: An empirical test of transaction cost analysis. *Journal of Law, Economics, and Organization, 4* (Fall), 121-139.

Kelly, H. H., & Thibaut, J. W. (1978). *Interpersonal relations: A theory of interdependence.* New York: John Wiley & Sons.

Kerlinger, F. N. (1986). *Foundations of Behavioral Research* (3rd ed.). Chicago, IL: Holt, Rinehart, and Winston, Inc.

Klein, S., Frazier, G. L., and Roth, G. (1990). A transaction cost analysis model of channel integration in international markets. *Journal of Marketing Research, 27* (May), 196-208.

Loehlin, J. C. (1992). *Latent variable models: An introduction to factor, path, and structural analysis*. Hillsdale, NJ: Lawrence Erlbaum Associates, Inc.

Macneil, I. (1980). *The new social contract*. New Haven, CT: Yale University Press.

Maney, K. (1999). Middlemen have nothing to fear despite scary word. *USA Today* (March, 24), Final Edition.

Mead, G. H. (1934). *Mind, self, and society: From the standpoint of a social behaviorist*. Chicago: University of Chicago Press.

Nunnally, J. C. (1978). *Psychometric theory* (2nd Edition). New York, NY: McGraw-Hill Inc.

Pease, P. (2000). Taking time to communicate effectively with technology. *Agency Sales Magazine, 30* (6), 68.

Peterson, R. A., Balasubramanian, S., & Bronnenberg, B. J. (1997). Exploring the implications of Internet for consumer marketing. *Journal of the Academy of Marketing Science, 25* (4), 329-346.

Quelch, J. A., & Takeuchi, H. (1981). Non-store marketing: Fast track or slow. *Harvard Business Review, 58*, 103-112.

Reynolds, J. (1997). Retailing in computer-mediated environments: Electronic commerce across Europe. *International Journal of Retail & Distribution Management, 25* (1), 29-38.

Reynolds, J., & Davies, R. L. (1988). *The development of teleshopping and teleservices*. Harlow, Essex: Longman.

Scheer, L. K., & Stern, L. W. (1992). The effect of influence type and performance outcomes on attitude toward the influencer. *Journal of Marketing Research, 29* (February), 128-42.

Stern, L. W., & El Ansary, A. I. (1988). *Marketing Channels* (3rd Ed.). Englewood Cliffs, NJ: Prentice-Hall, Inc.

Tanner, Jr., J. F., Hunt, J. B., & Eppright, D. R. (1991). The protection motivation model: A normative model of fear appeals. *Journal of Marketing, 55* (3), 36-46.

Thoits, P. A. (1992). On merging identity theory and stress research. *Social Psychological Quarterly, 54*, 101-112.

Turner, R. H. (1978). The role and the person. *American Journal of Sociology, 84*, 1-23.

Weiss, A. M., and Anderson, E. (1992). Converting from independent to employee salesforces: The role of perceived switching costs. *Journal of Marketing Research, 29* (February), 101-115.

Welbourne, T. M., Johnson, D. E., & Erez A. (1998). The role-based performance scale: Validity analysis of a theory-based measure. *Academy of Management Journal, 41* (5), 540-556.

Weitz, B., Castleberry, S. B., & Tanner, J. F. (2001). *Selling: Building Partnership*. Boston, MA: McGraw-Hill Inc.

Williams L. J., and Hollahan, P. J. (1994). Parsimony-based fit indices for multiple-indicator models: Do they work? *Structural Equation Modeling, 1* (2), 161-189.

Williamson, O. E. (1985). *The economic institutions of capitalism: Firms, markets, relational contracting*. New York: The Free Press.

The Fallacy of the Level Playing Field:
The Effect of Brand Familiarity
and Web Site Vividness
on Online Consumer Response

David A. Griffith
Clifton C. Gray

SUMMARY. The assertion that the web is a level playing field is examined employing cue utilization theory. This study examines the influence of the extrinsic cues of brand familiarity and web site vividness on consumer response (perceived retailer quality, believability and emotional response). The assertion that the web is a level playing field is founded on the belief that the extrinsic cue of web site vividness allows unfamiliar brands to compete against familiar brands. Results from this study indicate that although both extrinsic cues elicit a consumer response, the effects differ, thus challenging the level playing field argument. As such, this study provides for greater theoretical understanding of the recent collapse of many online retailers. Future directions for researchers and practitioners are discussed. *[Article copies available for a fee from The Haworth Document Delivery Service: 1-800-HAWORTH. E-mail address:*

David A. Griffith is Associate Professor of Marketing, Department of Marketing, College of Business Administration, C402g, University of Hawaii, 2404 Maile Way, Honolulu, HI 96822 (E-mail: griffith@cba.hawaii.edu). Clifton C. Gray is Programmer/Analyst, SiteMaster, Inc., 9731 East 54th Street, Tulsa, OK 74146 (E-mail: cgray@sitemaster.com).

[Haworth co-indexing entry note]: "The Fallacy of the Level Playing Field: The Effect of Brand Familiarity and Web Site Vividness on Online Consumer Response." Griffith, David A. and Clifton C. Gray. Co-published simultaneously in *Journal of Marketing Channels* (Best Business Books, an imprint of The Haworth Press, Inc.) Vol. 9, No. 3/4, 2002, pp. 87-102; and: *Internets, Intranets, and Extranets: New Waves in Channel Surfing* (ed: Audhesh Paswan) Best Business Books, an imprint of The Haworth Press, Inc., 2002, pp. 87-102. Single or multiple copies of this article are available for a fee from The Haworth Document Delivery Service [1-800-HAWORTH, 9:00 a.m. - 5:00 p.m. (EST). E-mail address: getinfo@haworthpressinc.com].

87

KEYWORDS. Online retailing, cue utilization theory, brand familiarity, web site vividness

The tremendous growth in online retailing was founded in part on the belief that through web site design an unknown retailer could effectively compete with any retailer, i.e., the web provided for a level playing field. However, the recent shakeout among online firms has brought to the forefront the importance of traditional retail fundamentals. Although the online environment has become increasingly competitive, as noted by the recent failure of many online retailers, it still offers one of the best opportunities for future growth for dot-com start-ups and brick and mortar retailers. Ernst & Young's 2001 Global Online Retailing report highlights the fact that online opportunities are not going away. As we begin the new century not only are more people buying online, but they are buying more. According to Ernst & Young (2001), although books, CDs and computers still dominate online sales, consumers are beginning to move into new categories, such as apparel, health and beauty products, sporting goods, toys and other consumer product categories. Thus, as retailers continue to develop online strategies to compete for growing consumer purchases, consideration must be given to the cues consumers use for evaluating retailers.

Cue utilization theory suggests that consumers use a wide variety of extrinsic and intrinsic cues to evaluate a retailer and its products. The level playing field argument suggests that web design elements alone are the key extrinsic cue that stimulates consumer response. Sealey (1999) suggests that in an online environment, branding is becoming less important as marketers move toward more directed, personalization techniques. However, the fallacy of the level playing field argument is that consumers use multiple extrinsic cues when evaluating an online retailer and its products. Although researchers have begun to theorize how the web influences online exchange (e.g., Alba, Lynch, Weitz, Janiszewski, Lutz, Sawyer and Wood 1997; Hoque and Lohse 1999; Palmer and Griffith 1998; Peterson, Balasubramanian and Bronnenberg 1997), little research has examined consumer evaluative cues. Given the importance of cue utilization to retailers, the conceptual and empirical study of this issue is an important area of inquiry. Managerially, given the significant performance implications of stimulating online consumer response, this is of interest to dot-com and brick and mortar retailers.

The purpose of this study is to provide a better understanding of the extrinsic cues used by consumers to evaluate online retailers. First, cue utilization theory is examined to provide a theoretical foundation for understanding online consumer response. Next, a series of hypotheses are presented theorizing the influence of the extrinsic cues of brand familiarity and web site vividness on consumer response. A method section specifies the sample, the pre-testing, stimuli development, construct measurements and procedures. An analysis section details the statistical methods used to test the hypotheses. Finally, the results, their theoretical and managerial implications, and a review of the limitations of this study along with directions for future research are addressed.

THEORETICAL FRAMEWORK

Cue utilization theory provides a framework for analyzing consumer response to online retail stimuli. Consumer research on cue utilization has demonstrated that a variety of product and product-related attributes serve as cues when consumers make product inferences (Cox 1967; Olson 1972, Rao and Monroe 1989). Cue utilization theorizes that an array of cues serve as surrogate indicators of quality to consumers (Cox 1967; Olson 1972; Rao and Monroe 1989). Cues such as odor, noise, color, package, brand name, price, as well as many other physical attributes, are used by consumers when evaluating retailers and their products (Olson 1972; Peterson 1977; Rao and Monroe 1989).

Cues are classified as extrinsic or intrinsic (Olson 1972; Rao and Monroe 1989). Extrinsic cues are product-related attributes such as brand, price and packaging, which are not part of the physical product (Leavitt 1954). Intrinsic cues represent the physical properties of the product, such as ingredients and nutritional value that are used by consumers in their assessment of product quality (Richardson, Dick and Jain 1994). The relative salience of extrinsic and intrinsic quality assessment depends on the analytical value (i.e., the degree to which consumers associate a given cue with quality) and confidence value (i.e., the degree to which consumers have confidence in their ability to use and judge that cue accurately (Cox 1967; Olson 1972). Research evidence suggests that consumers tend to use both extrinsic and intrinsic cues concurrently when evaluating quality (Jacoby, Olson and Haddock 1971; Szybillo and

Jacoby 1974). While both intrinsic and extrinsic cues are important, in examining the web as a level playing field, the issue becomes whether or not, when intrinsic cues (e.g., products and product descriptions) are held constant, extrinsic cues (e.g., brand familiarity, web site vividness, etc.) influence consumer response. As such, within this study, the focus is on the influence on consumer response of two key extrinsic cues: brand familiarity and web site vividness.

HYPOTHESES

Brand Familiarity

The influence of a brand is an important extrinsic cue in consumer evaluations of retailers, products, etc. (Rao and Monroe 1989; Hoyer and Brown 1990; Richardson et al. 1994; Schneider and Perry 2000; Ailawadi, Neslin and Gedenk 2001). A brand is much more than a simple identifier for consumers. Brands provide critical evaluative information relating to both the product and the retailer, conveying product attributes such as quality as well as organizational attributes, such as credibility and believability (Aaker 1996; Kapferer 1997). As such, brand familiarity (i.e., conceptualized here as when a consumer is familiar with a brand and has positive experiences with the brand) reduces consumer risks associated with purchasing a product. While these cognitive elements are important, brands also act to stimulate emotional response (Aaker 1996; Kapferer 1997). Emotional elements associated with a brand provide depth and richness from brand ownership and patronage (Aaker 1996). As such, brands familiar to a consumer, as opposed to unfamiliar brands, have an established set of cognitive and affective associations into which a consumer, when engaging a brand, considers. Given the complexity of a brand and its associations, it is theorized that the extrinsic cue of brand familiarity positively influences consumer perception of retailer quality and believability (i.e., the credibility given by the consumer to the content presented by the retailer online) as well as emotional response. More formally stated:

H1: Compared to consumers exposed to the unfamiliar brand web site, consumers exposed to the familiar brand web site will have:

a. higher quality perceptions related to the retailer.
b. higher believability of the retailer's claims.
c. a more positive emotional response related to the retailer.

Web Site Vividness

Media vividness is defined as "the representational richness of a mediated environment as defined by its formal features" (Steuer 1992, p. 81). As such, web sites can be conceptualized along a continuum of high to low vividness, determined by their media elements (Hoffman and Novak 1996; Srirojanant and Thirkell 1998). Dennis and Kinney (1998) argue that elements of web site design, such as vividness, are critical to a user's evaluation of information presented. Text only presentation is characteristic of low vivid web site design while multi-media presentations, integrating animated graphical images, audio, video, as well as text, are characteristic of highly vivid web site design.

Research suggests that higher levels of web site vividness provide a richer contextual environment for users to process information, thus stimulating them to higher consumer response (Baecker and Mandler 1991; Baecker, Grudin, Buxton and Greenberg 1995; Dennis and Kinney 1998; Morrison and Vogel 1998). For example, researchers have found that certain elements of web site design, such as animated images and icons, are more meaningful than simple text presentations and as such stimulate consumers to more actively process the information presented (Rogers 1989; Baecker and Mandler 1991; Molina 1997; Morrison and Vogel 1998) as well as creating a more entertaining environment that stimulates an emotional response. Underlying the level playing field argument is the belief that highly vivid web site designs appear more professional and as such, consumers viewing them perceive the retailer to be more credible, thus providing a halo-effect to consumer response, such as perceived retailer quality, believability and emotional response. More formally stated:

H2: Compared to consumers exposed to the low web site design, consumers exposed to the high web site design will have:

   a. higher quality perceptions related to the retailer.
   b. higher believability of the retailer's claims.
   c. a more positive emotional response related to the retailer.

Interaction of Brand Familiarity and Web Site Vividness

Brand has a significant influence in consumer evaluations of retailers, products, etc. (Hoyer and Brown 1990; Richardson et al. 1994; Schneider and Perry 2000; Ailawadi et al. 2001). Brand related research has demonstrated that brand often operates as a moderator for other extrinsic cues, such as price (Richardson et al. 1994). As such, it is theorized that brand is a moderator of web site vividness in relation to its influence on online consumer response. In this case, increased brand familiarity will enhance the online consumer response to highly vivid web site designs. Therefore, it is theorized that:

H3: The greater the brand familiarity and web site vividness of the retailer, the:

    a. higher the quality perceptions related to the retailer.
    b. greater the believability related to the retailer's claims.
    c. more positive the emotional response to the retailer.

METHOD

The study was designed to examine the effects of the extrinsic cues of brand familiarity and web site vividness on perceived retailer quality, believability and emotional response in order to investigate the level playing field argument. To explore this issue, the development of stimuli was necessary.

Product Category and Brand Selection

The selection of the product category to use in the study was based upon two principal considerations: (1) subjects should be familiar with the product category, to enhance evaluation, but should not be highly involved with it, to minimize brand loyalty influences; and (2) the product category should not be something that the subjects would have been likely to have examined online (to minimize pre-exposure bias). Iterative pre-testing with undergraduate students, examining over twenty product categories, indicated that pasta sauce was an appropriate category to use in this study (i.e., in terms of moderate product involvement, product category knowledge and lack of direct online experience).

Next, pasta sauce web sites were examined to establish a base model of web site design. High and low vivid web sites were developed for use in the study. To examine the influence of brand familiarity on consumer response a well-known and unknown brand were used. "Prego" exhibited moderate brand familiarity in pre-testing. When tested, 94.8 percent of subjects were familiar with "Prego," 78.4 percent had purchased

"Prego," 69.1 percent would purchase "Prego" again, but only 12.2 percent were brand loyal. To maintain similar country-of-origin effects, that might significantly influence consumer response to pasta sauce, the fictitious brand "Gratzi" was used.

Web Site Vividness

Web site vividness was manipulated through common graphical aesthetic techniques. The low vivid web site was largely text-based, with graphics depicting the products. The high vivid web site was also largely text-based, but used techniques such as drop shadows and image framing, to enhance the existing text and graphics (for a comparison of high and low executions see Figure 1). Color of the graphics was consistent across sites to minimize differences. Navigation in the low and high vivid web site designs was identical. Each site contained a list of available sauces (both meat and vegetable) and for those sauces, categorized by type of sauce (red or white) and type of dish (appetizers, pasta and rice, or main courses). The sites also offered a form for contacting the company, a standard legal statement, and a page for online purchasing (see Figure 2).

Subjects

One hundred and eighty-five undergraduate students were recruited from a marketing department subject pool as part of an online classroom exercise. The sample consisted of 68 female and 117 male students. Eighty-nine percent of the subjects were between 19 and 24 years of age with the remainder of subjects being between the ages of 25 and 35 years. Fifty percent of the subjects reported spending six or more hours online per week. Approximately 46 percent of subjects had shopped on-line, with 90 percent spending less than one hour shopping online per week. Ninety-five percent reported that they spend two or less hours per week shopping for food, with only 2.8 percent shopping for food online.

Procedure

A 2×2, between subjects research design was used with four treatment conditions (high brand familiarity-high vivid web site: n = 54, high brand familiarity-low vivid web site: n = 42, low brand familiar-

FIGURE 1. High and Low Vivid Web Sites

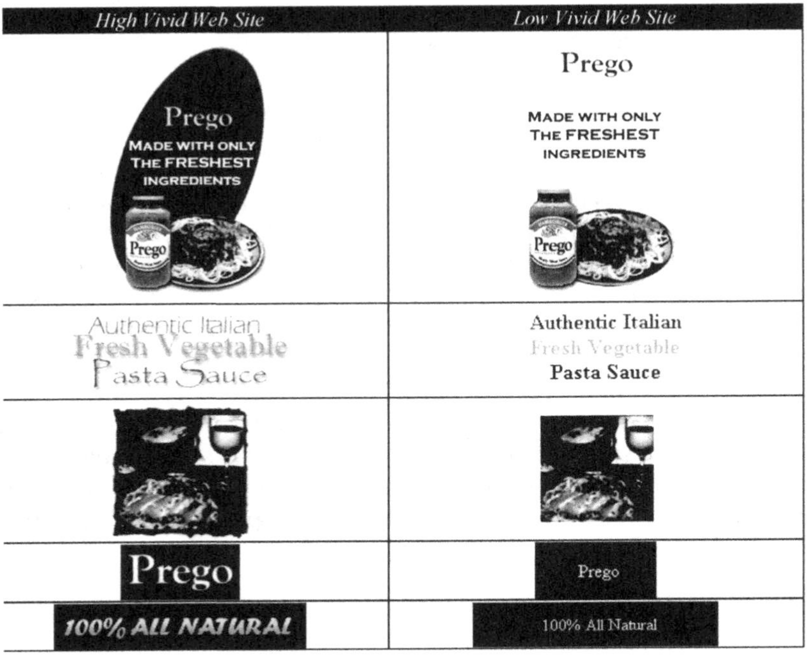

High Vivid Web Site
Low Vivid Web Site
Prego
MADE WITH ONLY THE FRESHEST INGREDIENTS
Prego
Prego
MADE WITH ONLY THE FRESHEST INGREDIENTS
Prego
Authentic Italian
Fresh Vegetable
Pasta Sauce
Authentic Italian
Fresh Vegetable
Pasta Sauce
Prego
Prego
100% ALL NATURAL
100% All Natural

FIGURE 2. Web Site Navigation Map

Main Page
Our Sauces
Recipes
Contact Us
Legal
Online Purchase
Red Sauce Recipes
White Sauce Recipes

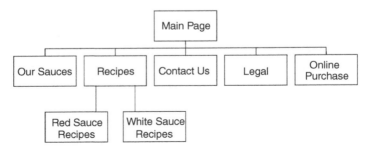

ity-high vivid web site: n = 47, low brand familiarity-low vivid web site: n = 36) (179 questionnaires were usable). Subjects were randomly assigned to each of the four treatment conditions, with each condition being contained in a separate room.

Independent administrators read instructions from a script describing the procedures to be followed. Administrators indicated that the subjects would be asked to evaluate the web site of an actual online retailer. Next, the administrator instructed subjects that prior to evaluating the retailer, questions regarding the product category, their familiarity with the web and then questions about the retailer and its products would need to be completed. Subjects were then asked to view the web site as they would normally view a web site at home. After viewing the web site, subjects were asked to turn off their computer screen and complete the questionnaire containing questions pertaining to the retailer, its products, site design and demographic data.

Measures

Perceived retailer quality refers to the overall evaluation of a retailer and its products. Perceived retailer quality was captured by a three-item, 7-point scale (cf. Dawson, Bloch and Ridgeway 1990). Subjects were asked to rate (1) the quality, (2) selection, and (3) prices of the products of the retailer from "1–Not at all satisfied" to "7–Very satisfied." Scale items were summed and then averaged. Coefficient alpha was .77 for this scale.

Believability refers to the consumer acceptance of arguments made by a retailer. Believability of the content presented on the web site was measured by a ten-item, 7-point semantic differential scale (cf. Beltramini 1988). Subjects were asked to rate if they felt that the web site was: (1) unbelievable-believable, (2) untrustworthy-trustworthy, (3) unconvincing-convincing, (4) unreasonable-reasonable, (5) dishonest-honest, (6) questionable-unquestionable, (7) inconclusive-conclusive, (8) unauthentic-authentic, (9) not credible-credible, and (10) unlikely-likely. Scale items were summed and then averaged. Coefficient alpha was .93 for this scale.

Emotional response refers to the consumer's affective mood state resulting from a stimulus. Emotional response to the web site was measured using a four-item, 7-point semantic differential scale (cf. Yi 1990). Subjects were asked to rate if the web site made them feel: (1) extremely unhappy-extremely happy, (2) displeased-pleased, (3) uncomfortable-comfortable, and (4) bad-good. Scale items were summated and then averaged. Coefficient alpha was .90.

ANALYSIS AND RESULTS

Means and standard deviations of the treatment conditions are presented in Table 1. The hypotheses were examined using 2-way MANOVA. MANOVA results indicated no significant interaction effects (see Table 2). Lacking significant interaction effects, main effects were explored.

Main Effects

Hypothesis 1a theorized that the high brand familiarity treatment would stimulate a higher perception of retailer quality than low brand

TABLE 1. Means, Standard Deviations

	High Brand Familiarity	Low Brand Familiarity
High Web Site Vividness		
Quality	5.15	4.73
	(0.95)	(1.06)
Believability	5.61	5.09
	(0.94)	(1.19)
Emotion	4.87	4.84
	(1.04)	(1.08)
Low Web Site Vividness		
Quality	4.75	4.40
	(1.03)	(0.86)
Believability	5.53	5.10
	(0.80)	(1.01)
Emotion	4.41	4.44
	(0.98)	(0.82)

TABLE 2. MANOVA Results

Source	SS	df	MS	F	Sig
Level of Brand Familiarity					
Quality	6.41	1	6.41	6.67	.011
Believability	9.94	1	9.94	10.01	.002
Emotion	0.00	1	0.00	0.00	.994
Level of Web Site Vividness					
Quality	5.90	1	5.90	6.14	.014
Believability	0.04	1	0.04	0.04	.852
Emotion	8.10	1	8.10	8.10	.005
Brand Familiarity ×					
Vividness Interaction					
Quality	0.05	1	0.05	0.06	.814
Believability	0.09	1	0.09	0.09	.761
Emotion	0.02	1	.020	.020	.888
Total					
Quality	4,293.56	179			
Believability	5,310.31	179			
Emotion	4,081.33	179			

familiarity treatment. Results support H1a ($F_{1,175} = 6.67$, p = .011). Hypothesis 1b theorized that a retailer with higher brand familiarity would stimulate greater believability than a retailer with a lower familiar brand. Results support H1b ($F_{1,175} = 10.01$, p = .002). H1c stated that a retailer with high brand familiarity would stimulate a more positive emotional response from consumers than a retailer with low brand familiarity. Results do not support H1c ($F_{1,175} = 0.00$ p = .994).

Hypothesis 2a theorized that a high vivid web site would result in a higher perception of retailer quality than a low vivid web site. Results support H2a ($F_{1,175} = 6.14$, p = .014). Hypothesis 2b theorized that a high vivid web site design would stimulate higher believability than a low vivid web site. Results do not support H2b ($F_{1,175} = 0.04$, p = .852). H2c stated that a more vivid web site design would result in a more positive emotional response from consumers than a low vivid web site. Results support H2c ($F_{1,175} = 8.10$, p = .005).

Interaction Effect

H3a,b,c theorized that an interaction between brand familiarity and web site vividness would exist. Results do not support H3a,b,c in relation to perceived retailer quality (H3a: $F_{1,175} = 0.06$, p = .814), believability (H3b: $F_{1,175} = 0.09$, p = .761) or emotional response (H3c: $F_{1,175} = 0.20$, p = .888).

DISCUSSION

The objective of this study was to examine the influence of the extrinsic cues of brand familiarity and web site vividness on perceived retailer quality, believability and emotional response. Results indicate that both brand familiarity and web site vividness are important extrinsic cues determining online consumer response. However, results did not support the interaction of the two extrinsic cues on online consumer response.

Findings indicate that higher levels of brand familiarity resulted in higher perceived retailer quality and believability of the content of the online retailer's web site. This suggests that online consumers use brand as an extrinsic cue in their evaluation of an online retailer's offering. This finding is both consistent with prior research on brand as an extrinsic cue, as well as challenges the legitimacy of the level playing field argument that would suggest the lessening importance of branding online. This study demonstrates that, holding information content constant, brand familiarity significantly influences the cognitive evaluation (perceived retailer quality and believability) of the online retailer and its claims. Further, brand familiarity was found not to influence the emotional response of consumers. This result is surprising in that research has found there to be an affective element related to brands (e.g., Aaker 1996; Kapferer 1997). As such, one would expect this relationship to exist in the online context as well as in the offline context. However, this finding should be interpreted with caution as it may result from the product category in which this experiment was conducted (i.e., pasta sauce), rather than the retail context (online vs. offline).

The results also indicate that web site vividness plays an important role as an extrinsic cue for consumers. Both perceived retailer quality of material contained within the site as well as emotional response was positively influenced by web site vividness. This finding supports the belief that web site design is an important extrinsic cue in stimulating online consumer response. Although believability was not influenced by web site vividness, the ability of web site vividness to serve as an extrinsic cue to enhance the perceived retailer quality suggests that consumers use web site vividness in their evaluation of the retailer and its products. Also, the affective stimulation elicited through vividness is consistent with prior research in human computer interaction that suggests that more vivid media elements stimulate consumers affectively. As such, these findings indicate that the employment of vivid web site design can enhance the consumer perception of a retailer.

Managerially, the results of this study highlight the importance of online branding and web site vividness in stimulating a positive consumer response. The results of this study demonstrate that highly vivid web site design can improve consumer response to an online retailer, thus lending support to the level playing field argument. However, the level playing field argument is founded, to some extent, on the belief that branding is not an important extrinsic cue in the online retail environment. Clearly, the results supporting the importance of brand familiarity in the online retail context challenge this argument. Given the importance of branding online, managers may find their online efforts more effective if resources are expended in first developing greater brand familiarity. This is not to suggest an either/or decision in resource allocation between building brand familiarity and web site vividness, but rather that those retailers with low brand familiarity may wish to increase investment in the development of brand familiarity to stimulate consumer response.

Clearly, brand management will continue to grow in its importance in the online arena. Retailers with well-established brands, such as JCrew and Wal-Mart, can leverage their brand familiarity online (Evans and Wurster 1999). For retailers with high brand familiarity, the issue becomes one of developing highly vivid web sites to enhance emotional response from consumers. Brand management may be the differentiating factor that determines who can reach critical mass online, thus succeeding.

Limitations and Future Research Directions

As with all studies, this study has its limitations. First, laboratory settings have the potential to distort the levels of variables and therefore may not generate results that are typical of consumer responses in the external environment. However, given the controlled setting of a laboratory experiment and the randomization of subjects to treatment conditions, it can be reasonably assumed that while external validity was compromised, differences across groups are attributable to the treatment conditions (i.e., manipulation of level of brand familiarity and web site vividness). As with any laboratory study, future research needs to be conducted in a more natural setting to establish external validity.

Second, only a single product category (i.e., pasta sauce) within a single industry (i.e., packaged food products) was examined. As such, this study provides a relatively small test of the influence of extrinsic cues on online consumer response. Future research should address this issue within a broader range of product categories and industries. For example, researchers could examine the influence of brand familiarity and web site vividness within the business-to-business marketplace or within the consumer electronics product category.

Further, several research issues should be addressed as researchers continue to develop and test cue utilization theory in an online context. For example, comparisons between extrinsic cue effectiveness between print and online media could be examined. As the web provides for a more interactive environment than print media, it could be theorized that extrinsic cue effectiveness may vary across media. Also, the exploration of the conditions in which the two extrinsic cues of brand familiarity and web site vividness interact would be of benefit to understanding this complex area of retailing.

In summary, this study provides a number of contributions to online retailing by examining the extrinsic cues of brand familiarity and web site vividness under the framework of cue utilization theory. Next, this study provides substantial evidence that brand management in the online environment is key to stimulating consumer response. Further, the findings suggest that web site vividness significantly influences consumer response. Clearly, the findings challenge the idea of the level playing field suggesting that as more mass-market consumers enter the marketplace, brand familiarity and web site vividness will become increasingly important.

REFERENCES

Aaker, David A. (1996) *Building Strong Brands*, New York: Free Press.

Ailawadi, Kusum L., Scott A. Neslin and Karen Gedenk (2001), "Pursuing the Value-Conscious Consumer: Store Brands Versus National Brand Promotions," *Journal of Marketing*, 65 (1), 71-89.

Alba, Joseph W., John Lynch, Barton Weitz, Chris Janiszewski, Richard Lutz, Alan Sawyer and Stacy Wood (1997), "Interactive Home Shopping: Consumer, Retailer, and Manufacturer Incentives to Participate in Electronic Marketplaces," *Journal of Marketing*, 61 (3), 38-53.

Baecker, R.M. and R. Mandler (1991), "Bringing Icons to Life," in *Human Factors in Computing Systems, CHI'91 Conference Proceedings*, S.P. Robertson, G.M. Olson, and J.S. Olson (eds.), pp. 1-6, New York, NY: ACM Press.

_____ J. Grudin, W.A.S. Buxton, and S. Greenberg (1995), *Readings in Human Computer Interaction; Toward the Year 2000*. Morgam Kauftnan, San Francisco, CA.

Beltramini, Richard F. (1988), "Perceived Believability of Warning Label Information Presented in Cigarette Advertising," *Journal of Advertising*, 17 (1), 26-32.

Cox, Donald F. (1967), "The Sorting Rule Model of the Consumer Product Evaluation Process," in *Risk Taking and Information Handling in Consumer Behavior*, D.F. Cox, ed., Boston: Harvard University.

Dawson, Scott, Peter H. Bloch and Nancy M. Ridgeway (1990), "Shopping Motives, Emotional States and Retail Outcomes, *Journal of Retailing*, 66(Winter), 408-427.

Dennis, Alan R. and Susan T. Kinney (1998), "Testing Media Richness Theory in the New Media: The Effects of Cues, Feedback and Task Equivocality," *Information Systems Research*, 9 (3), September, 256-274.

Evans, P. and T. S. Wurster (1999), "Getting Real about Virtual Commerce," *Harvard Business Review*, (November-December), 85-94.

Ernst & Young (2001), *Global Online Retailing*, Ernst & Young LLP.

Hoffman, Donna L., and Thomas P. Novak (1996), "Marketing in Hypermedia Computer Mediated Environments: Conceptual Foundations," *Journal of Marketing*, 60 (3), 50-68.

Hoque, Abeer Y. and Gerald L. Lohse (1999), "An Information Search Cost Perspective for Designing Interfaces for Electronic Commerce," *Journal of Marketing Research*, 34 (3), 387-394.

Hoyer, Wayne D. and Steven P. Brown (1990), "Effects of Brand Awareness on Choice for a Common, Repeat-Purchases," *Journal of Consumer Research*, 17 (2), 141-148.

Jacoby, Jacob, Jerry Olson and Rafael Haddock (1971), "Price, Brand Name and Product Composition Characteristics as Determinants of Perceived Quality," *Journal of Applied Psychology*, 55(December), 570-579.

Kapferer, Jean-Noel (1997), *Strategic Brand Management*, Second Ed., London: Kogan Page.

Leavitt, Harold J. (1954), "A Note on Some Experimental Findings about the Meaning of Price," *Journal of Business*, 27(July), 205-210.

Molina, Alfonso (1997), "Issues and Challenges in the Evolution of Multimedia: The Case of the Newspaper," *Futures*, 29 (3), 193-222.

Morrison, Joline and Doug Vogel (1998), "The Impacts of Presentation Visuals on Persuasion," *Information & Management*, 33 (3), 125-135.

Olson, Jerry C. (1972), "Cue Utilization in the Quality Perception Process: A Cognitive Model and Empirical Test," doctoral dissertation, Purdue University.

Palmer, Jonathan W. and David A. Griffith (1998), "Information Intensity: A Paradigm for Understanding Web Site Design," *Journal of Marketing Theory & Practice*, 6 (3), 38-42.

Peterson, Robert A. (1977), "Consumer Perceptions as a Function of Product, Color, Price and Nutrition Labeling," in *Advances in Consumer Research*, Col. 4, W.D. Perreault, Jr., ed. Atlanta: Association for Consumer Research, 61-63.

_____ Sridhar Balasubramanian and Bart J. Bronnenberg (1997), Exploring the Implications of the Internet for Consumer Marketing, *Journal of the Academy of Marketing Science*, 25 (4), 329-346.

Rao, Akshay R. and Kent B. Monroe (1989), "The Effect of Price, Brand Name, and Store Name on Buyers' Perceptions of Product Quality: An Integrative Review," *Journal of Marketing Research*, 26 (3), 351-357.

Richardson, Paul S., Alan S. Dick and Arun K. Jain (1994), "Extrinsic and Intrinsic Cue Effects on Perceptions of Store Brand Quality," *Journal of Marketing*, 58 (4), 28-36.

Rogers, Y. (1989), "Icons at the Interface: Their Usefulness," *Interacting with Computers*, 1, 295-315.

Schmitt, B. and A. Simonson (1997), *Marketing Aesthetics*, New York: The Free Press.

Schneider, G.P. and J.T. Perry (2000), *Electronic Commerce*, Cambridge: Thomson Learning. 2000.

Sealey, Peter (1999), "How E-Commerce Will Trump Brand Management," *Harvard Business Review*, (July-August), 171-176.

Srirojanant, Sirinuch, and Peter Cresswell Thirkell (1998), "Relationship Marketing and its Synergy with Web-based Technologies," *Journal of Market Focused Management*, 3 (1), 23-46.

Steuer, Jonathan (1992), "Defining Virtual Reality: Dimensions Determining Telepresence," *Journal of Communication*, 42 (4), 73-79.

Szybillo, George J. and Jacob Jacoby (1974), "Intrinsic vs. Extrinsic Cues as Determinants of Perceived Product Quality," *Journal of Applied Psychology*, 59(February), 74-78.

Yi, Youjae (1990), "Cognitive and Affective Priming Effects of the Context for Print Advertisements," *Journal of Advertising*, 19 (2), 40-48.

The Impact of Organizational and Environmental Factors on the Implementation of Internet-Based Marketing Channels

Niels Peter Mols

SUMMARY. This article presents a framework for understanding the implementation of Internet-based marketing channels. This process includes the activities from the time before a firm first considers using the Internet as a marketing channel until it is fully implemented. Based on data from a survey among 353 Danish manufacturers it is found that different factors are important in the implementation of different dimensions of Internet-based marketing channels. For instance top management support and knowledge of IT are the most important factors driving the implementation of the Internet for presentation of the firm, opening hours, and product information, whereas willingness to cannibalize and Internet market maturity are the most important factors driving the adoption of home pages for

Niels Peter Mols is Associate Professor, Department of Management, University of Aarhus.

Address correspondence to: Niels Peter Mols, Afdeling for Virksomhedsledelse, Universitetsparken 350, Aarhus Universitet, 8000 Aarhus C, Denmark (E-mail: nmols@econ.au.dk).

The author gratefully acknowledges the research assistance of Lennart Sand Kirk and the financial support from the Aarhus University Research Foundation, research grant # F-1999-SAM-1-10.

[Haworth co-indexing entry note]: "The Impact of Organizational and Environmental Factors on the Implementation of Internet-Based Marketing Channels." Mols, Niels Peter. Co-published simultaneously in *Journal of Marketing Channels* (Best Business Books, an imprint of The Haworth Press, Inc.) Vol. 9, No. 3/4, 2002, pp. 103-131; and: *Internets, Intranets, and Extranets: New Waves in Channel Surfing* (ed: Audhesh Paswan) Best Business Books, an imprint of The Haworth Press, Inc., 2002, pp. 103-131. Single or multiple copies of this article are available for a fee from The Haworth Document Delivery Service [1-800-HAWORTH, 9:00 a.m. - 5:00 p.m. (EST). E-mail address: getinfo@haworthpressinc.com].

receiving orders. The data also indicates that the importance of the factors affecting the implementation of new channels may differ between the stages of implementation. *[Article copies available for a fee from The Haworth Document Delivery Service: 1-800-HAWORTH. E-mail address: <getinfo@haworthpressinc.com> Website: <http://www.HaworthPress.com> © 2002 by The Haworth Press, Inc. All rights reserved.]*

KEYWORDS. Electronic marketing channels, the Internet, drivers of and barriers to implementation

INTRODUCTION

The economic literature on marketing channels has been concerned with understanding the relationship between channel efficiency and (a) the use of inventories, (b) the use of search intermediaries (e.g., Bucklin, 1966, 1970), and (c) the use of vertical integration (Anderson and Weitz, 1986; Anderson and Coughlan, 1987). Building on micro economic theory these models have been of a static comparative nature, and they have been the basis for normative models for the design of customer-driven distribution channels (Stern and Sturdivant, 1987; Stern et al., 1996; Rangan et al., 1992). A few of the models have noted the important aspect of implementation and suggested ways to facilitate implementation of new distribution channels by gaining acceptance from the management team (Stern et al., 1996), and others have pointed to the barriers for change in distribution channels (e.g., McCammon, 1971; Weiss and Anderson, 1992). However, no empirical studies have focussed on the implementation of new marketing channels and incorporated a process perspective in the analysis of their changes. In this respect marketing channels research are not different from research into other elements of marketing strategies and thus it corroborates the observations made by Noble and Mokwa (1999). They found that implementation has not been the direct focus of much marketing research and from a review of the implementation research in marketing they concluded that prior research has three limitations. Most of it has only provided tangential reference to the implementation stage, it has ignored manager-level factors, and its generalizability has not been tested.

These observations are surprising considering that implementation is important for at least three reasons: First, proper and well coordinated implementation is necessary for most strategies to become successful. Second, fast implementation is necessary when responding to changes in the environment, which may threaten the firms' market position. Third, if implementation of new marketing systems consists of several distinct stages with their own characteristics and conditions, then different factors are likely to be important for advancing through these stages. If research ignores the different stages it may overlook factors which are important at only a few of the implementation stages and it may generate unstable results (Krumwiede, 1998).

It is the purpose of this article to analyse the implementation of Internet-based marketing channels. It will be illustrated how an analysis may be carried out by use of a stage model and it will be shown how a number of organizational, product-related, technological and environmental factors interact with the implementation of new Internet-based marketing channels. The article asks two questions:

1. Are different factors important in implementing changes in different marketing functions?
2. Are different factors important on different stages of the implementation of a change in a marketing function?

In order to answer these two questions the article first develops a framework for explaining the implementation of new marketing channels. The development of the theoretical framework has three components. First, we identify a number of factors which may affect the implementation of new Internet-based marketing channels. Secondly, Internet-based marketing channels are divided into eight different functions which describe some of the activities that may be performed by an Internet-based marketing channel. Thirdly, the implementation process is divided into five distinct stages of implementation. These three components are then integrated into a framework and two tentative hypotheses are suggested. In the last part of the article the two hypotheses are tested. The method is described and the results of a survey among Danish producer firms are presented. Finally, the theoretical and managerial implications are discussed.

FACTORS AFFECTING THE IMPLEMENTATION OF NEW MARKETING CHANNELS

Environmental and Technological Factors

Bucklin (1966) argues that the starting point for changes in distribution channels are innovations resulting in new marketing technology and changes in consumer wants. This starts an adaptation process where the existing channel gravitates towards the new normative channel. The adaptation process is described by changes in the functional and institutional structure. This is manifested by functional substitutions, vertical integration and disintegration, and the entering of new firms, the exit of old firms, mergers and acquisitions. However, Anderson et al. (1997) note that distribution systems are usually rigid and stable, and Weiss and Anderson (1992) conclude from their study that many firms do not change their distribution channels in the frictionless way suggested by normative theory and that the conversion process is connected with substantial inertia. They find that distribution channels change slowly and firms wanting to convert from one type of distribution channel to another often face resistance, conflicts and confused customers. Bucklin (1966) also notes that the adaptation is not likely to happen overnight because of barriers and temporal constraints. The temporal constraints arise because the decision makers have the existing distribution channel as a starting point for the changes. Therefore, the existing distribution channel also influences the adaptation in the distribution channel structure.

McCammon (1971) identifies five different barriers to change of marketing channel structures. First, reseller solidarity has the consequence that resellers prefer and support traditional distribution channel practices and existing institutional relationships. Secondly, entrepreneurial values differ among firms. Large firms are argued to be growth oriented and hence more entrepreneurial than smaller firms, which are less ambitious and have more static expectations. Thirdly, organizational rigidity exists because of established norms and positions in the organisation, risk aversion and sunk costs which many firms prefer to recover before they change their procedures. However, McCammon (1971) also emphasises that in case an innovator is penetrating the firm's core market, then it is likely to be more innovative and react much more quickly to the threat. Fourthly, the firm's channel position can be that of an insider or an outsider, and McCammon (1971) argues that it is the outsiders, which innovate and are the initiators of major structural changes. Finally, customers are heterogeneous and not all the different customer segments are likely to accept and react equally rapid to innovations in distribution channels.

Thus, from traditional distribution channel literature there seems to be at least four major external factors, which may influence the implementation of new marketing channels combining Internet-based channels with traditional dealer-based channels: (1) existing *distributors* and their reactions to new channels (Bucklin, 1966, McCammon, 1971), (2) *competi-*

tor activities (McCammon, 1971), (3) changes in customer wants, i.e., *market maturity* and the *market uncertainty* connected with the changes in customer wants (Bucklin, 1966, McCammon, 1971), and (4) the new marketing technology (Bucklin, 1966). Some of the factors discussed in relation to Internet-based marketing are the problems connected with *Internet payments* and *Internet contracts* (Turban et al., 2000).

Organizational Factors

Earlier studies on innovation have emphasised the direct relationship between *management support* and the implementation and adoption of innovations and new marketing strategies (Damanpour, 1991; Noble and Mokwa, 1999), and much of the literature on new service development emphasises management support for innovations and implementation of changes as the most important prerequisite for new service development (Drew, 1995a, 1995b). In their comprehensive review article Johne and Storey (1998) also identify top management and their provision of a clear corporate vision, resources and help as one of the most important factors for successful new service development. For example, Drew (1995a) found that lack of senior management support was a major barrier to new product development in financial institutions, and Drew (1995b) argued that the speed with which a new service is brought to the market is critical to the competitive advantage and that top level commitment is one of the most important factors for success.

The innovations and IT literature has also emphasised the *ownership/involvement* of users as being important for gaining acceptance and decreasing resistance to change and thus ensuring implementation success (Gales and Mansour-Cole, 1995; Ives and Olson, 1984). In their review of the user involvement research Ives and Olson (1984) identify the following advantages of user involvement and participation: (1) Better assessment of user requirements, avoidance of features, which are unacceptable or unimportant, and better knowledge of the organization where the system is to be used. (2) Better user understanding and realistic expectation to an IT system. (3) Establish ownership and commitment by users and decrease resistance to change. Thus, involvement should have the effect of achieving a better quality of the Internet channel, of generating acceptance of the new channel among the employees, and thus facilitating the adoption of the channel. Some of the organizations which have experiences with the implementation of new IT technology for use by their customers are libraries. Based on experiences from these organizations, Farley et al. (1998), for example, emphasise such elements as staff involvement and the resulting staff commitment in order to successfully implement a new technology. They note that without the cooperation of the staff then an attempt to initiate change will be difficult and probably futile. However, if the staff feel a sense of ownership towards a change then they will try to make it successful. The literature on implementation of, for example accounting systems, have also emphasised the positive effect from creating a sense of ownership among other groups of employees than the systems developers from the accounting departments, though the empirical results have been mixed (e.g., Krumwiede, 1998).

Several articles mention the importance of a technology *champion* in organizations (Gatian et al., 1995). For example, Howell and Higgins (1990) describe the importance of the champions of technological innovation. In their review of earlier research results they note that the success of technological innovations is dependent on individuals who contribute to the innovation by actively and enthusiastically promoting its progress. These champions take ownership of the idea, they identify it as their own and are willing to risk their position and prestige to ensure its success. Leonard-Barton (1992) also emphasises the important challenge to make empowered individuals channel their energy towards corporate aims. Hence, it seems that in order to become a success, it is important that either one or more among the management team or another powerful employee pay attention to the new marketing channels. Only by such attention it is possible to capture the attention of others and make them committed to these marketing innovations.

The degree of *centralization* is also likely to influence the innovation process in the firms. As mentioned by Thompson (1965) centralized decision making may hamper innovations. On the other hand, participation may facilitate innovation (Damanpour, 1991). In centralized firms the employees do not have the autonomy to make their own decisions. Decisions have to be approved by senior staff before action can be taken. Even small Internet strategy issues have to be referred to someone in the corporate office for a final decision, and resistance in part of the organization may stop an Internet project. If, however, a firm is decentralized and the employees empowered to take their own decisions regarding the Internet then lack of top management support or resistance from other parts of the organization may not be an important barrier to the development of new Internet-based systems. Thus, decentralization may approximate effective internal markets, where a high degree of autonomy lets the decision makers compete against each other. In such decentralized organizations decision makers staking on Internet-based marketing channels do not have to worry about cannibalizing other managers investments (cf. Chandy and Tellis, 1998).

Besides the involvement and support from groups in the firm an implementation effort may also be affected by the availability of essential *IT knowledge* internally in the firm. Non-educated employees and a lack of training will result in a lack of knowledge about the importance of the Internet, its opportunities, and in what way it may be used by the firm. For example, Burke and Litwin (1992) argue that individual skills and abilities are important for successful change effort. Also Damanpour (1991) mentions that technical knowledge resources may be expected to positively influence the implementation of an innovation. Therefore it seems that IT knowledge is an important factor when studying the implementation of Internet-based marketing channels.

This suggests that another five variables: (1) top management support, (2) involvement of employees, (3) Internet champions, (4) centralization, and (5) IT knowledge, may be important drivers or barriers of the implementation of Internet-based marketing channels.

Market Orientation

From the marketing literature it has been suggested that *market orientation* and *future market orientation* may also influence the innovativeness of a firm and thus the adoption of new Internet-based marketing channels. According to Kohli and Jaworski (1990) a market orientation is comprised of three elements: market intelligence, intelligence dissemination, and customer responsiveness. If customers want and value Internet-based marketing channels then market oriented firms will have registered this, spread the information to the organization and reacted to it. However, market oriented firms may take their starting point in the existing segments in the market. If these segments are stable then they are usable for designing the distribution channels (cf. Stern et al., 1996). However, the customer segments identified may be unstable, and new technology may change the relationship between costs and service output. Thus, firms which are oriented towards the present market may end up with channels which fall behind the needs and wants of their customers.

This is not likely to happen for a future market oriented firm. A future-oriented firm will be interested in future profit, future customer segments and competitors. It is a measure of how alert the decision makers are to new technologies and changes among competitors and customers. A future-market focus is defined by Chandy and Tellis

(1998, p. 479) as "the extent to which a firm emphasizes future customers and competitors relative to current customers and competitors." A firm oriented towards the present and the past will be unwilling to cannibalize existing investments, whereas a future-oriented firm will be willing to do so (Chandy and Tellis, 1998). It will not be attached to investments made in products, employees or channels which will not be able to generate profit in the future. Furthermore, a future-oriented firm will be interested in those customers who will be the most attractive customers in a year or more from now, whereas a firm oriented to the past and present will be attached to its customers and focus on serving present customers' needs and wants without preparing for how these needs and wants may develop. This is in accordance with the findings that future-oriented firms are more innovative (Kitchell, 1995). The previous suggests that both a firm's market orientation and a firm's future market orientation may influence the implementation of new Internet-based marketing channels.

Existing Investments

New research in product innovations suggest that *specialized investments* and *willingness to cannibalize* may be important factors affecting the adoption of innovations in a firm (Chandrashekaran et al., 1999; Chandy and Tellis, 1998).

Many firms have invested huge resources in their existing distribution channels. They have built relationships with different distributors or have opened stores, hired employees, taught them to work with their products and services and implemented effective organizational routines (Stern et al., 1996; Weiss and Anderson, 1992). These investments may be channel specific investments that is, they have limited or no value if these channels cease to exist (cf. Williamson, 1996). Traditional firms on the consumer market have invested in stores, the promotion of the stores, their employees at the stores, and the procedures used for their day-to-day activities–all of which are investments which will be of no or lower value if Internet-based distribution channels become the most important distribution channel. As noted by Chandy and Tellis (1998) such investments may be the result of years of hard work on the part of the managers. They may develop a strong commitment to these investments, which can lead to sub-optimal or irrational decisions. Thus, Staw (1981) found that individuals may commit new and additional resources to a losing course of action. Hence, in order to protect the channel specific investments, the managers may be hesitant to introduce competing channels.

Chandy and Tellis (1998, p. 475) define *willingness to cannibalize* as the "extent to which a firm is prepared to reduce the actual or potential value of its investments." As mentioned a firm often has a huge amount of resources invested in its distribution channels. A firm which is willing to cannibalize existing distribution channels does not avoid certain channels in order not to render employees or existing stores redundant. It does not wait until it is forced by competitors to innovate and introduce new channels but it allocates resources in order to handle the new channels and to integrate them in the existing organization. As noted by Chandy and Tellis (1998), the willingness to cannibalize present investments is a desirable trait, because it promotes innovation and is necessary for the long-term survival of the firm. It may, however, hurt short-term profit, because new distribution channels may result in old distribution channels becoming unprofitable.

Firm Size

It has also been suggested that *firm size* may have an influence on the adoption of Internet-based marketing channels. For example, Pavitt (1990) argues that several factors may explain why technological discontinuities, such as new electronic distribution channels, can co-exist with institutional continuities, i.e., the continued existence of a number of firms. Large established firms have specialized functions which are provided with resources enabling them to accumulate skills. Furthermore, these departments may gain experience in integrating a number of skills from different functional areas, thus being able to manage even very complex projects, such as developing and implementing an Internet-based marketing channel. Finally these large firms often have both the time and resources to thoroughly explore the implications of new technology. They are able to build prototypes of Internet-channels, test them, and link them to the existing business system without having to move into large scale commercialization unless they seem to become a success. Smaller firms have less slack and lack the resources to be the first to develop, introduce and promote new distribution channels.

These arguments are congruent with Srirojanant and Thirkell's (1998) hypothesis, which states that the size of business is positively correlated with the level of web-site interactivity for that business. They, however, found the opposite relationship between size and adoption of web-site interactivity and speculated that managers in smaller businesses were more ambitious concerning the implementation of interactive web-sites. Thus, their experience was in accordance with those of Chandy and Tellis (1998), who ended their review of research on firm size and radical innovation by concluding that no consensus about the role of firm size have been reached.

Products

For the effect of different product characteristics only anecdotal evidence exists. Highly *complex products* with a large degree of customization will be related to extensive information exchange. It will be difficult to describe the products on a few pages on the Internet. Some products will also be connected with attributes which will have to be experienced by the buyers in order for them to fully understand and appreciate them. This suggests that in case of highly complex and customized products there will be a greater need for face-to-face interaction between the buyer and the seller. For example, Smith (1999, p. 164) speculates that " . . . it's not clear that customers would be willing to spend several thousand dollars for a fine designer outfit they haven't touched or tried on . . . my sense is that most customers would not. On the other hand, for customers who are seeking many fashion basics, gifts, or tried-and-true products, the Internet may provide a more efficient shopping experience than the physical store." In time this may be possible by virtual meeting on the Internet–however, the technology is not developed to an extent to which it has the same quality as a face-to-face meeting.

Brand names may contain all necessary information for the consumers in order to decide whether or not to buy a product. However, some of the manufacturers, who own strong brand names, will be concerned with protecting these brand names and with maintaining their exclusivity. Therefore they will be likely to continue to rely on exclusive distribution, and hence the stronger the brand names the more likely the manufacturers will be to use the Internet for all other functions than selling of their products. This suggests that both product complexity and the presence of strong brand names may have an effect on the adoption of Internet-based marketing channels.

HYPOTHESES AND FRAMEWORK

New marketing channels may carry out different marketing functions. Internet-based channels usually involve the presentation of the firm, its products, its employees, opening hours, etc. The home pages may also promote two-way communication with the customers in the form of e-mails, feedback from the customers, discussion groups, news-letters, ordering information, etc., and more integrated systems may connect the home page and the electronic communication between the firm and the customers with the other systems in the firm (e.g., Greaves et al., 1999; Srirojanant and Thirkell, 1998; Evans and Wurster, 1999). Some of the functions of an Internet-based marketing channel may be:

1. Presentation of the firm: Pictures of the company, its age, its financial statements, etc.
2. Presentation of its employees, opening hours, addresses, telephone numbers, etc.
3. Product descriptions, pictures, specifications, etc.
4. E-mail communication with the customers.
5. Receiving orders via the home page.
6. Using the home page for obtaining customer feedback.
7. Home page integrated with other systems in the company, for example logistic system, customer complaint handling, accounting system, etc.
8. Gathering of information about the customers' use of home page.

These eight functions represent different tasks for the marketing channel. These different tasks require different skills and will influence the relationships with customers and competitors differently. For example, the gathering and interpretation of information about specific customers' use of a firm's home page require different skills than are needed for developing a home page with a picture of the firm, a verbal presentation of the firm and its history and a detailed technical presentation of the firm's products. Some of the functions are more complex and require the involvement of several departments and employees inside the firm. In order to implement these functions it may be necessary to have involved employees, Internet champions and top management support. This may not be required for the less complex functions such as presentation of the firm. The manufacturer may find it crucial to respond to a competitor's implementation of two-way communication with the customers, integrated systems and data capturing, whereas if competitors only use the Internet for providing information to their customers then the manufacturer may not feel a pressure to offer the same information via the Internet. Finally, a manufacturer, who is only using the Internet for presentation of the firm and its products, is not likely to generate as much conflict and cannibalization of existing channels as is a manufacturer implementing an advanced integrated Internet-based sales and marketing channel through which the customers are able to order products. Thus, specialized investments, willingness to cannibalize, and distributor reactions are likely to have a large impact on the implementation of functions which involve Internet-based sales and interaction with the customers.

Thus, the drivers of and barriers to establishing a simple homepage will be different from the drivers of and barriers to establishing a homepage which is integrated with the other systems in the firm such as the logistical system. This results in the first hypothesis:

H1. Different factors are important in the implementation of different functions of Internet-based marketing channels such as presentation of the firm, communication by e-mail, integration with other systems in the firm, etc.

In 1947 Lewin suggested to describe change as consisting of three stages which he called unfreezing, moving, and freezing. Several researchers have built on this work in both organizational research (Armenakis and Bedeian, 1999), research on implementation of IT systems (Cooper and Zmud, 1990) and on the implementation of activity-based costing (Krumwiede, 1998). Kwon and Zmud (1987) developed Lewin's (1947) three stage model into a model with six stages: initiation, adoption, adaption, acceptance, routinization, and infusion. This model was then used by Cooper and Zmud (1990) to study the implementation of material requirements planning systems focussing on how certain variables had a different effect on different implementation stages. In his study of implementation of activity-based costing, Krumwiede (1998) expanded the six stages into a ten stage model: not considered, considering, considered then rejected, approved for implementation, analysis, getting acceptance, implemented then abandoned, acceptance, routine system, and integrated system. Despite their application in other business areas these stage models have not been used in marketing research nor in the study of marketing channels.

Inspired by Krumwiede (1998) a model with five stages has been chosen for this framework: not considered, considering, planned, getting implemented, and implemented/successfully implemented. This stage model with fewer stages has been chosen primarily because it is simple enough to be used as a scale in a questionnaire and thus be combined with the different marketing functions. In this article we suggest that the implementation of new electronic marketing channels is similar to the implementation of other kinds of IT-based systems and organizational changes in the respect that the drivers and barriers will vary from stage to stage in the implementation. Hence, different factors will be associated with the "not considered" stage and "the considering stage" than with the stages "implemented" and "successfully implemented." This results in the second hypothesis:

H2. The importance of the factors affecting the implementation of new channels vary between the different stages of the implementation.

Hypotheses 1 and 2 are the basis for the tentative framework suggested for the study of implementation of new marketing channels. This framework is outlined in Figure 1. The left side of the Figure contains the drivers and barriers to the implementation of Internet-based Marketing Channels and the right side describes the implementation stages of changes in a marketing channel function. The horizontal arrows signify that each of the drivers and barriers may affect the transition from one stage of change to another. In the next sections the framework will be used in an empirical study testing hypotheses 1 and 2.

METHOD

The survey was conducted in October and November 1999 by mail questionnaire to a cross-section of 772 Danish manufacturing firms. The manufacturers were rather small firms with 48.9% having 20 to 49 employees, 26.4% having between 50 and 99 employees, 13.9% having 100 to 199 employees, and 11.6% having 200 or more employees. They were from the following industries: Publishing, data hardware and software, health products, radio and television, clothing, toys, optics, pumps and compressors, paper, refrigerators and kitchen appliances, communication equipment, and office supply; and no single industry grouping comprised more than one fourth of the respondents. The results presented in Table 3 containing the correlations for the test of hypothesis 1 were computed several times using different combinations of industries. No noteworthy differences between the correlation coefficients were found, which indicates that the results are not biassed because of the different industries selected for the sample. Table 1 shows

FIGURE 1. A Stage Model for Implementation of Changes in Marketing Functions

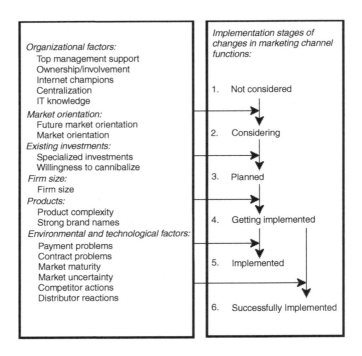

the stages of implementation of Internet-based sales and marketing in the surveyed organizations.

The questionnaire was pre-tested and one key informant was identified in each firm by the use of the database CD-Direct. To increase the response rate the questionnaire was sent together with a cover letter with a handwritten signature. As an incentive the respondents were promised to receive a small report on the results of the study. After a reminder with a fresh copy of the questionnaire and a return envelope 353 answers were received. The respondents were all marketing managers and had on average 9 years of experience in the organization and on average 6 years in their present position. Only 6.4% of the respondents had less than one year of experience in the organization, and 8.5% of the respondents had less than one year in their present positions.

Following Armstrong and Overton (1977) several tests were made to ensure that the respondents were representative of the sample and

TABLE 1. Implementation Stages of Internet-Based Sales and Marketing

	Not considered	Considering	Planned	Getting implemented	Implemented	Successfully implemented
Use of the Internet:	%	%	%	%	%	%
Presentation of the firm	2	11	6	18	39	24
Opening hours, addresses, etc.	8	10	6	14	43	20
Product information	2	10	6	18	41	22
E-mail communication with the customers	4	8	5	10	39	34
Receiving orders via home page	21	33	11	14	15	7
Customer feedback via home page	13	29	11	12	24	12
Home page integrated with other systems	32	37	15	9	5	3
Information capturing: use of home page	22	27	15	14	17	6
Note: 336 < n < 352						

thereby the population. By use of Pearsons χ^2-test non-respondents were compared to respondents and respondents answering before receiving a reminder were compared to respondents answering after receiving a reminder. Using a one percent level of significance only one difference was found on any of the questions in the questionnaire and none were found on the measures of industry and firm size. This indicates that non-response bias is not a problem.

RESULTS

Measures

The measures were developed primarily by literature search. The questionnaire was pretested with the aim of ensuring that the respondents understood and were able and willing to answer the questions. The variables used in the study were formed by combining scale items to produce a summed score. The wording of the items, the mean, and the standard deviation are shown in the Appendix. The internal consistency was evaluated by the use of Cronbach's coefficient alpha. The diagonal in Table 2 contains Cronbach's alpha for the constructs used. For eleven of the variables Cronbach's alpha are above 0.60. Only three variables have Cronbach's alphas between 0.51 and 0.59. Though some of the measures need refinement, the reliability seems acceptable given the exploratory nature of the study. An exploratory and a confirmatory fac-

TABLE 2. Correlation Matrix–The Factors Affecting the Implementation of New Marketing Channels

Kendall's tau-b	1	2	3	4	5	6	7	8	9	10	11	12	13	14	15	16	17	18
1. Top management support	0.84																	
2. Ownership	0.27c	0.51																
3. Champions	0.29c	-0.14c	0.52															
4. Centralization	0.01	0.00	0.05	0.77														
5. IT knowledge	0.33c	0.32c	0.05	-0.10c	0.80													
6. Future market orientation	0.16c	0.08b	0.08a	-0.01	0.17c	0.59												
7. Market orientation	0.23c	0.19c	0.04	0.05	0.20c	0.27c	0.66											
8. Specialized investments	-0.25c	-0.25c	0.03	0.03	-0.27c	-0.12c	-0.15c	0.75										
9. Willingness to cannibalize	0.33c	0.20c	0.14c	0.01	0.28c	0.13c	0.11c	-0.30c	0.82									
10. Firm size	-0.01	0.03	-0.04	-0.11c	0.14c	-0.01	0.03	-0.06	-0.02	na								
11. Product complexity	-0.07a	0.01	-0.15c	0.01	-0.01	0.06	0.09b	0.12c	-0.21c	0.02	0.76							
12. Strong brand names	0.09b	0.06	0.08b	-0.04	0.07	0.10b	0.03	-0.03	-0.01	0.02	0.02	na						
13. Internet payment	-0.13c	-0.05	-0.03	0.11c	-0.13c	-0.08a	0.04	0.13c	-0.15c	-0.10c	0.09b	-0.04	na					
14. Internet contracts	-0.16c	-0.10b	-0.06	0.07a	-0.12c	-0.08b	0.02	0.17c	-0.18c	-0.08b	0.11c	0.00	0.63c	na				
15. Market maturity	0.26c	0.02	0.21c	-0.02	0.18c	0.11c	0.03	-0.14c	0.32c	0.04	-0.25c	0.06	-0.14c	-0.16c	0.75			
16. Market uncertainty	-0.22c	-0.07a	-0.13c	0.08a	-0.17c	-0.09b	-0.03	0.19c	-0.25c	-0.10b	0.08b	-0.07	0.33c	0.32c	-0.28c	0.72		
17. Competitors	0.07	-0.01	0.12c	-0.04	0.07	0.00	-0.06	0.01	0.14c	0.06	-0.17c	-0.02	0.03	0.01	0.36c	-0.10b	0.70	
18. Distributor reactions	-0.13c	-0.15c	0.02	0.11b	-0.08	0.06	0.00	0.22c	-0.22c	0.01	0.09a	0.02	0.10a	0.18c	-0.11b	0.18c	-0.10a	0.89

Note: a: $p < 0.10$ b: $p < 0.05$ c: $p < 0.01$ The diagonal contains Cronbach's coefficient alphas

tor analysis also indicated an acceptable reliability and validity of the measures except for the discriminant validity of two pairs of variables. The analysis could not discriminate between Involvement and Internet champions, and Market maturity could not be separated from Competitors.

Table 2 reports the correlations between all the factors affecting the implementation of Internet-based marketing channels. Many of the correlations are insignificant and only one correlation exceeds 0.4, which is an indication that most of the variables may be manipulated relatively independently of each other. Nomological validity is supported by several correlations in Table 2. Firstly, the results show that the higher the specialized investments, the lower the management support. This supports the proposition that management becomes attached to the investments that they have made. Secondly, the positive correlation between willingness to cannibalize and future market orientation is also in accordance with expectations (cf. Chandy and Tellis, 1998), since a high degree of willingness to cannibalize is an indication that past investments are regarded as less important than the future market conditions. Thirdly, the positive correlation between willingness to cannibalize and management support is in accordance with the expectation that managers who are aware of the advantages connected with new distribution channels and are also willing to cannibalize the existing channels if necessary (Chandy and Tellis, 1998).

It is noteworthy that the measures of firm size is insignificantly correlated with all but four of the independent variables. Thus, with respect to the independent variables there seem to be almost no differences between the smallest and the largest manufacturing firms. This is an indication that the respondents do not perceive the manipulation of the drivers and the overcoming of the barriers to Internet-based marketing to be easier for the largest firms to handle than for the smaller firms.

Test of Hypothesis 1

Table 3 reports the first-order correlations between the factors affecting the implementation of Internet-based marketing channels and the actual implementation of different marketing channel functions. This is used for testing the first hypothesis. The analysis presented in Table 3 shows that top management support ($0.22 < \tau < 0.32$), IT knowledge ($0.22 < \tau < 0.32$), willingness to cannibalize ($0.17 < \tau < 0.33$), market uncertainty ($0.13 < \tau < 0.33$) and market maturity ($-0.22 < \tau < -0.13$)

TABLE 3. Correlations Between Marketing Channel Functions and the Factors Affecting Their Implementation

	Presentation of the firm	Opening hours, adresses, etc.	Product information	E-mail communication with customers	Receiving orders via home page	Customer feedback via home page	Home page integrated with other systems	Information capturing: use of home page
Top management support	0.28c	0.32c	0.27c	0.25c	0.22c	0.25c	0.26c	0.25c
Ownership/ involvement	0.21c	0.15c	0.18c	0.16c	-	0.15c	0.13b	-
Champions	-	0.13b	-	-	-	-	-	0.16c
Centralization	-	-	-	-	-	−0.13b	-	-
IT knowledge	0.35c	0.31c	0.32c	0.31c	0.22c	0.26c	0.27c	0.28c
Future market orientation	0.15c	0.12b	0.14c	0.12b	-	-	0.15c	0.13b
Market orientation	0.12b	-	-	0.11b	-	-	-	0.13b
Specialized investments	−0.19c	−0.20c	−0.20c	−0.20c	−0.16c	−0.17c	−0.23c	-
Willingness to cannibalize	0.17c	0.21c	0.21c	0.29c	0.33c	0.22c	0.33c	0.17c
Firm size	0.12b	0.12b	-	-	-	-	-	0.11b
Product complexity	-	-	-	-	−0.17c	-	−0.14b	-
Strong brand names	0.15c	0.14b	0.18c	-	-	0.15c	-	0.19c
Internet payment	-	-	-	-	-	-	−0.13b	-
Internet contracts	-	-	-	-	-	-	−0.14b	-
Market maturity	0.13b	0.17c	0.15c	0.15c	0.32c	0.22c	0.33c	0.20c
Market uncertainty	−0.18c	−0.20c	−0.18c	−0.16c	−0.13b	−0.14c	−0.22c	−0.15c
Competitors	-	-	-	-	0.23c	0.14c	0.18c	-
Distributor reactions*	-	-	-	−0.17b	−0.22c	−0.24c	-	-

Note: Kendall's tau-b first-order correlation coefficients   a: Only $195 < n < 212$;   b: $p < 0.01$;   c: $p < 0.001$

are significantly correlated with all the eight functions. Thus, these variables have some variation in the correlation coefficients, however, a number of the other items had larger variations in their correlation coefficients across the eight functions. For example, competitor activities and distributor reactions were significantly correlated ($p < 0.001$) with the use of the Internet for receiving orders and feedback from the customers and with having a home page which is integrated with other systems in the firm, whereas they had insignificant correlations with the other functions. Problems with Internet-based payments and contracts were only significantly correlated with home pages integrated with other systems in the firm. Thus, the results indicate that payment and contractual problems may primarily serve as a barrier to the adoption of integrated systems. Championing was significantly correlated with "information capturing," but has insignificant correlations with most other functions. Centralization was only significantly correlated with customer feedback via the home page and ownership, future market focus, market orientation, specialized investments, firm size, product complexity, and brand names all had some significant and some insignificant correlations. Thus, the results in Table 3 support hypothesis 1.

However, the results presented in Table 3 are the partial correlations, and in order to fully evaluate the results a simultaneous estimation is needed for each marketing channel function. Thus, for each of the eight functions a logistic regression with ordinal response was estimated (cf. Table 4). The SAS-system was used for the estimations, the marketing channel functions were set to be the dependent variables, and a stepwise model selection method was used with p-values for entering and exiting the model set at $p = 0.1$ (SAS Institute Inc., 1990, pp. 1071-1126). The results presented in Table 4 were validated by the SAS-system's probit analysis (SAS Institute Inc., 1990, pp. 1325-1350). The results from the probit analysis were almost the same as with the logistic regression procedure. Four variables–ownership/involvement, future market orientation, market orientation and Internet contracts–were not related to any of the functions performed by the Internet-based marketing channels and were omitted from Table 4. For all eight models a Score test and a -2 Log Likelihood test (-2 LOG L) are reported. These two statistics give tests for the joint significance of the independent variables (SAS Institute Inc., 1990, p. 1075) and shows that the combined effects of the variables entered into the models are significant ($p < 0.01$). Because only 231 out of 353 respondents reported that they used dealers for distributing their products and thus, were able to supply the answers related to distributor reactions this variable was initially eliminated from the analysis. When it was entered it reduced the number of usable observations from $280 < n < 291$ to $178 < n < 183$. The results showed that distributor reactions entered the regression when "receiving orders via home page" ($p = 0.04$ and $\beta = -0.17$) and "customer feedback via home page" ($p = 0.0003$ and $\beta = -0.29$) were the dependent response variables.

TABLE 4. Logistic Regression with Ordinal Response: Marketing Channel Functions and the Factors Affecting Their Implementation

	Presentation of the firm	Opening hours, adresses, etc.	Product information	E-mail communication with customers	Receiving orders via home page	Customer feedback via home page	Home page integrated with other systems	Information capturing: use of home page
Top management support	0.18c	0.22c	0.16b	-	-	-	-	0.16b
Champions	-	-	-	-	-	-	-	0.16b
Centralization	-	-	-	-	-	−0.17c	-	−0.10a
IT knowledge	0.37c	0.24c	0.32c	0.31c	0.17b	0.21c	0.19c	0.33c
Specialized investments	-	−0.12a	−0.14b	-	-	−0.17c	−0.16b	-
Willingness to cannibalize	-	-	-	0.36c	0.27c	-	0.19b	-
Firm size	-	-	-	-	-	-	0.11a	-
Product complexity	0.11a	-	-	-	−0.12a	-	-	-
Strong brand names	0.16c	0.16c	0.22c	0.11a	-	0.15b	-	0.11a
Internet payment	-	-	-	-	-	-	-	0.16b
Market maturity	-	-	-	-	0.25c	0.25c	0.19b	-
Market uncertainty	−0.11a	−0.17b	-	-	-	-	−0.13a	−0.14b
Competitors	-	-	-	-	0.13b	-	0.17b	-
Model fit:								
−2 Log L-test for β = 0	p < 0.01	p < 0.01	p < 0.01	p < 0.01	p < 0.01	p < 0.01	p < 0.01	p < 0.01
Score-test for β = 0	p < 0.01	p < 0.01	p < 0.01	p < 0.01	p < 0.01	p < 0.01	p < 0.01	p < 0.01
Score-test: proportional odds assump	p = 0.05	p = 0.08	p = 0.02	p = 0.13	p < 0.01	p = 0.04	p = 0.14	p = 0.95

Note: Standardized parameter estimates a: $p < 0.10$; b: $p < 0.05$; c: $p < 0.01$;
The SAS-system's LOGISTIC procedure was used. Response scale was coded: 1 = successfully implemented, 2 = implemented, 3 = getting implemented, 4 = planned, 5 = considering and 6 = not considered.

If we compare the results from Table 3 with the results in Table 4 we see a large reduction in the number of significant correlations. This indicates that multi-collinearity exists among the independent variables and that the results should be interpreted with caution. IT knowledge is the only factor which significantly influences all eight functions (Table 4).

The effect from the other factors varies between the different functions and thus the results provides support for hypothesis 1, which stated that different factors are important in the implementation of different dimensions of Internet-based marketing channels.

Test of Hypothesis 2

Using a one per cent level of significance the Score-test for the proportional odds assumption could not reject that the slope functions are parallel for each stage for all but one marketing channel function (cf. Table 4). This indicates that for seven of the eight marketing channel functions the effect from the drivers and barriers are not different as the implementation progresses from one stage to the next stage. The Score-test for the proportional odds assumption was significant (p < 0.01) for the function "receiving orders via home page" and hence it was decided to analyse the results between each of the six stages for this function. This is done in Table 5, which reports the results from applying the stage model to this function.

Table 5 shows that the importance of the factors affecting the implementation of "receiving orders via home page" vary between the different stages of the implementation. However, only for a few variables the correlation coefficients change from being positive to being negative or reverse as the implementation progresses through the six stages. This indicates that ignoring the different stages of implementation of new innovations are not likely to result in seriously misleading or contradictory results. In other words, such studies may be used for trying to identify important factors affecting the implementation of new Internet-based marketing channels.

In order to take the step from not considering to considering receiving orders via the homepage market maturity ($\tau = 0.32$) and willingness to cannibalize ($\tau = 0.30$) are the most important drivers but also top management support, Internet champions, and competitors' actions are important drivers at these stages. A high product complexity is the only significant barrier ($\tau = -0.25$). The progression from the considering stage to the planning stage are positively related to willingness to cannibalize and market maturity and negatively related to specialized investments and problems with Internet contracts. The progression from planning stage to the implementation stage is positively related to top management support, champions and firm size, and negatively related to centralization. Thus, it seems that whereas the initial stages are associated with external drivers, the internal

TABLE 5. Receiving Orders via the Home Page

	Kendall's tau-b: Implementation stages					Kruskal-Wallis test: p-values
	1-2	2-3	3-4	4-5	4-6	
Top management support	0.15b	-	0.17a	-	-	0.0001
Ownership/involvement	-	-	-	-	-	0.0562
Champions	0.11a	-	0.16a	-0.16a	-	0.1003
Centralization	-	-	-0.16a	-	-0.17a	0.1172
IT knowledge	-	-	-	0.16a	0.22b	0.0001
Future market orientation	-	-	-	-	-	0.4348
Market orientation	-	-	-	-	-	0.6580
Specialized investments	-	-0.15b	-	-	-	0.0028
Willingness to cannibalize	0.30c	0.17b	-	-	-	0.0001
Firm size	-	-	0.21b	-0.18b	-0.22b	0.0557
Product complexity	-0.25c	-	-	-	-	0.0001
Strong brand names	-	-	-	-	-	0.1253
Internet payment	-	-	-	0.24c	-	0.1049
Internet contracts	-	-0.13a	-	0.17a	-	0.0312
Market maturity	0.32c	0.23c	-	-0.17a	0.20a	0.0001
Market uncertainty	-	-	-	-	-	0.0088
Competitors	0.28c	-	-	0.16a	-	0.0001
Distributor reactions	-	-	-	-	-0.23a	0.0021

Note: Kendall tau-b first order correlations; a: $p < 0.10$ b: $p < 0.05$ c: $p < 0.01$
Implementation scale: 6 = successfully implemented, 5 = implemented, 4 = getting implemented, 3 = planned, 2 = considering and 1 = not considered.

drivers become more important when facing the difficult task of getting from planning to implementation. The progression from getting implemented to either the implemented or the successfully implemented stages are positively associated with IT knowledge and negatively associated with firm size. Thus, it seems that smaller firms have it easier in getting new Internet-based marketing and sales finally implemented than large firms, which may have a more complex and time consuming implementation process. Compared to the firms describing their implementation as being successful the firms not being successful in their implementation seem to lack champions ($\tau = -0.16$), seem to have more problems with the payment ($\tau = 0.24$) and contracts ($\tau = 0.17$), seem to be on less mature markets ($\tau = -0.17$), and seem to be more driven by competitor activities ($\tau = 0.16$). On the other hand, the firms with a successful implementation are less centralized ($\tau = -0.17$), are operating on more mature markets ($\tau = 0.20$), and experience less distributor reactions ($\tau = -0.23$).

DISCUSSION AND CONCLUSIONS

Stern and Sturdivant (1987) contend that of all marketing decisions facing the firms those which concern the design of distribution systems are the most far reaching because to change them is very resource demanding and time consuming, and hence firms have to take great care when designing their distribution system. This view seems to have led to a focus on design of distribution channels, while implementation problems have been ignored. This paper, however, develops a model for studying the implementation of new marketing channels. Based on the model, two hypotheses are proposed and tested with data from Danish manufacturers.

It was shown that different factors are important in the implementation of different dimensions of Internet-based marketing channels–presentation of the firm, opening hours, product information, e-mail communication with the customers, receiving orders via the home page, home page integrated with other systems in the firm and the capturing of information about customers' use of the firm's home page. Thus, future research should be careful when choosing the functions they want to study because results generated from a study of one function may not be immediately generalizable to other aspects of Internet-based marketing channels. However, the study also indicated that IT knowledge is essential for getting all dimensions of Internet-based marketing channels implemented. Thus, managers and policy makers wanting to facilitate the implementation of Internet-based marketing should ensure that knowledge of the Internet and skills necessary for the creation of home pages are widely available in the workforce. It is also noteworthy that if the manufacturers expect distributor reactions, in case they start selling directly to the consumers from Internet-based channels, then the manufacturers will hesitate to implement the new channels. This indicates that existing retailers will be able to hamper the implementation of Internet-based marketing channels, if they are able to credibly signal that they will replace the manufacturers implementing Internet-based marketing channels.

The study also found weak indications that the importance of the factors affecting the implementation of new marketing channels vary between the different stages of their implementation. We focussed on the Internet used for receiving orders via the firms' home pages and found that willingness to cannibalize and market maturity were important for making the firms consider Internet-based marketing channels. However, in getting from plans to a successful implementation IT knowledge in the firm, decentralized decision making, and the avoidance of distributor reactions were important.

Still, very little is known about the consequences of adding an electronic distribution channel to an existing channel network. This article focussed on the effect of both internal and environmental factors. Future studies could include other variables like the power of the actors in the channel and the strategies considered for managing channel conflict. Especially, more empirical research is needed on the electronic marketing channels and their interaction with the existing distribution systems. The results may be different if firms in monopoly positions and with no close substitutes are surveyed. In that case top management support, specialized investments, willingness to cannibalize, and existing channels will probably be more important than market maturity, market uncertainty, and competitor actions for explaining the implementation of dual marketing channels.

The results indicate an interaction between design decisions and the implementation process. However, we have not been able to identify any empirical studies of the interaction between design and implementation considerations in marketing channels. Thus, this seems to be a neglected topic, which deserves more attention by marketing researchers.

REFERENCES

Aiken, M. and Hage, J. (1968), "Organizational Independence and Intra-Organizational Structure," *American Sociological Review*, 33 (December), 912-930.

Anderson, E. and Weitz, B.A. (1986), "Make-or-Buy Decisions: Vertical Integration and Marketing Productivity," *Sloan Management Review*, Spring, 3-19.

Anderson, E. and Coughlan, A.T. (1987), "International Market Entry and Expansion via Independent or Integrated Channels of Distribution," *Journal of Marketing*, 51 (1), 71-82.

Anderson, E.; Day, G.S. and Rangan, V.K. (1997), "Strategic Channel Design," *Sloan Management Review*, 38 (4), 59-69.

Armenakis, A.A. and Bedeian, A.G. (1999), "Organizational Change: A Review of Theory and Research in the 1990s," *Journal of Management*, 25 (3), 292-315.

Armstrong, J.S. and Overton, T.S. (1977), "Estimating Non-Response Bias in Mail Surveys," *Journal of Marketing Research*, 14 (3), 396-402.

Bucklin, L.P. (1966), *A Theory of Distribution Channel Structure*, IBER Special Publications, Berkeley.

Bucklin, L.P. (1970), *"A Normative Approach to the Economics of Channel Structure,"* in Bucklin, L.P., (Ed.), Vertical Marketing Systems, Scott, Foresman and Company, Glenview, 159-175.

Burke, W. and Litwin, G. (1992), "A causal model of organizational performance and change," *Journal of Management*, 18, 523-545.

Chandrashekaran, M.; Mehta, R.; Chandrashekaran, R. and Grewal, R. (1999), "Market Motives, Distinctive Capabilities, and Domestic Inertia: A Hybrid Model of Innovation Generation," *Journal of Marketing Research*, XXVI, (February), 95-112.

Chandy, R.K. and Tellis, G.J. (1998), "Organizing for Radical Product Innovation: The Overlooked Role of Willingness to Cannibalize," *Journal of Marketing Research*, 35 (4), 474-487.

Cooper, R.B. and Zmud, R.W. (1990), "Information Technology Implementation Research: A Technological Diffusion Approach," *Management Science*, 36 (February), 123-139.

Damanpour, F. (1991), "Organizational innovation: A meta-analysis of effects of determinants and moderators," *Academy of Management Journal*, 34 (3), 555-590.

Drew, S. (1995a), "Strategic benchmarking innovation practices in financial institutions," *International Journal of Bank Marketing*, 13 (1), 4-16.

Drew, S. (1995b), "Accelerating innovation in financial services," *Long Range Planning*, 28 (4), 11-21.

Evans, P. & Wurster, T.S. (1999), "Getting Real About Virtual Commerce," *Harvard Business Review*, (November-December), 85-94.

Farley, T., Broady-Preston, J. and Hayward, T. (1998), "Academic libraries, people and change: a case study of the 1990s," *Library Management*, 19 (4), 238-251.

Gales, L. and Mansour-Cole, D. (1995), "User involvement in innovation projects: Towards an information processing model," *Journal of Engineering and Technology Management*, 12, 77-109.

Gatian, A.W.; Brown, R.M. and Hicks, J.O. (1995), "Organizational innovativeness, competitive strategy and investment success," *Journal of Strategic Information Systems*, 4 (1), 43-59.

Greaves, C.; Kipling, P. & Wilson, T.D. (1999), "Business use of the World Wide Web, with particular reference to UK companies," *International Journal of Information Management*, 19, 449-470.

Gupta, A.K. (1987), "SBU Strategies, Corporate-SBU Relations, and SBU Effectiveness in Strategy Implementation," *Academy of Management Journal*, 30 (September), 477-501.

Howell, J.M. and Higgins, C.A. (1990), "Champions of Technological Innovation," *Administrative Science Quarterly*, 35 (2), 317-341.

Ives, B. and Olson, M.H. (1984), "Use Involvement and MIS Success: A Review of Research," *Management Science*, 30 (3), 586-603.

Johne, A. and Storey, C. (1998), "New service development: a review of the literature and annotated bibliography," *European Journal of Marketing*, 32 (3/4), 184-251.

Kitchell, S. (1995), "Corporate Cultur, Environmental Adaptation, and Innovation Adoption," *Journal of the Academy of Marketing Science*, 23 (3), 195-205.

Kohli, A.K. and Jaworski, B.J. (1990), "Market Orientation: The Construct, Research Propositions, and Managerial Implications," *Journal of Marketing*, 54 (2), 1-18.

Kohli, A.K.; Jaworski, B.J. and Kumar, A. (1993), "MARKOR: A Measure of Market Orientation," *Journal of Marketing Research*, XXX (November), 467-477.

Krumwiede, K.R. (1998), "The Implementation Stages of Activity-Based Costing and the Impact of Contextual and Organizational Factors," *Journal of Management Accounting Research*, 10, 239-277.

Kwon, T.H. and R.W. Zmud (1987), "Unifying the fragmented models of information systems implementation." In *Critical Issues in Information Systems Research*, Edited by R.J. Boland and R. Hirscheim. New York, NY: John Wiley.

Leonard-Barton, D. (1992), "Core Capabilities and Core Rigidities: A Paradox in Managing New Product Development," *Strategic Management Journal*, 13 Special Issue, 111-125.

Lewin, K. (1947), "Frontiers in group dynamics," Human Relations, 1, 5-41.

McCammon, B.C. (1971), "Alternative Explanations of Institutional Change and Channel Evolution," in W.G. Moller and D.L. Wilemon eds., *Marketing Channels– A Systems Viewpoint*, R.D. Irwin, Homewood, pp.134-145.

Noble, C.H. and Mokwa, M.P. (1999), "Implementing Marketing Strategies: Developing and Testing a Managerial Theory," *Journal of Marketing*, 63 (October), 57-73.

Pavitt, K. (1990), "What We Know about the Strategic Management of Technology," *California Management Review*, 23 (3), 17-26.

Rangan, V., Menezes, M. & Maier, E. (1992), "Channel Selection for New Industrial Products: A Framework, Method, and Application," *Journal of Marketing*, 56 (3), 69-82.

SAS Institute Inc. (1990), *SAS/STAT User's Guide*, Version 6, Fourth Edition, Volume 2, Cary, NC: SAS Institute Inc.

Smith, R.A. (1999), in "Retailing: Confronting the challenges that face bricks-and-mortar stores," *Harvard Business Review*, (July-August), 159-168.

Srirojanant, S. and Thirkell, P.C. (1998), "Relationship Marketing and its Synergy with Web-based Technologies," *Journal of Market-Focused Management*, 3 (1), 23-46.

Staw, B.M. (1981), "The Escalation of Commitment to a Course of Action," *Academy of Management Review*, 6 (4), 577-587.

Stern, L.W.; El-Ansary, A. and Coughlan, A.T. (1996), *Marketing Channel*, Prentice-Hall, London.

Stern, L.W. and Sturdivant, F.D. (1987), "Customer-Driven Distribution Systems," *Harvard Business Review*, 65 (4), 34-41.

Thompson, V.A. (1965), "Bureaucracy and innovation," *Administrative Science Quarterly*, 22, 28-45.

Turban, E.; Lee, J.; King, D. and Chung, H.M. (2000), *Electronic Commmerce. A Managerial Perspective*, Prentice-Hall, Upper Saddle River, NJ.

Weiss, Allen M. and Erin Anderson (1992), "Converting from Independent to Employee Salesforces: The Role of Perceived Switching Costs," *Journal of Marketing Research*, 29 (1), 101-115.

Williamson, O.E. (1996), "*The Mechanisms of Governance*," Oxford University Press, NY.

APPENDIX

MEASURES

Scale format:				
1 **Strongly disagree**	**2** **Disagree**	**3** **Neutral**	**4** **Agree**	**5** **Strongly agree**

Construct name:	Items used:
Top management support Mean = 11.7 S.D. = 2.8	Top management supports the exploitation of the Internet. The Internet receives a lot of attention from top management. The use of the Internet is linked to the rest of the firm's strategy.
Involvement Mean = 9.9 S.D. = 2.4	We need employees who will take responsibility for the development of the Internet in this firm. (Reversed) There is a significant resistance against the development of the Internet in this firm. (Reversed) There is a need for more involvement of employees in order to be able to implement the use of the Internet. (Reversed)
Internet champions Mean = 7.7 S.D. = 1.7	Central employees' support for the use of the Internet has a great importance. Internet champions have a clear impact on Internet development in this firm.
IT knowledge Mean = 9.6 S.D. = 3.1	We possess the necessary knowledge of the Internet. We have plenty of employees with knowledge of the Internet. We can design and update a home page ourselves.
Future market orientation (adapted from Kohli, Jaworski, and Kumar, 1993; Chandy and Tellis, 1998) Mean = 12.6 S.D. = 2.6	This firm gives more emphasis to customers of the future, relative to current customers. We are quick to adapt to changes in our business. We are oriented more toward the future than the present. In this industry it is important to be first with new initiatives.
Market orientation (based on Kohli and Jaworski, 1990) Mean = 12.5 S.D. = 2.0	Our firm makes a lot of effort to have up-to-date information about our markets. The employees have a good understanding of our customers' needs. We often adapt to the wants of our customers.
Centralization (adapted from Aiken and Hage, 1968; Gupta, 1987; Chandy and Tellis, 1998) Mean = 10.6 S.D. = 2.8	Decisions regarding the Internet are taken by top management. Even small Internet related decisions need to be approved by the management team. It is important for the management team to have a large influence on the use of the Internet in this firm.

APPENDIX (continued)

Scale format:				
1 **Strongly disagree**	**2** **Disagree**	**3** **Neutral**	**4** **Agree**	**5** **Strongly agree**
Construct name:	**Items used:**			
Specialized investments (adapted from Anderson and Weitz, 1992) Mean = 17.5 S.D. = 5.2	It is difficult to integrate the existing technology with the new Internet technology. Our knowledge of sales and marketing cannot be applied to the exploitation of the Internet. Many of our current operating procedures cannot be applied to the new Internet technology. Our logistical system is badly suited for Internet-based sales and marketing. Our IT-systems are outdated. The expenses for IT in connection with adoption of Internet-based commerce are high. Our present sales and marketing activities cannot be applied with an Internet-based sales and marketing system.			
Willingness to cannibalize (adapted from Chandy and Tellis, 1998) Mean = 17.9 S.D. = 5.4	We can easily change our organizational scheme to fit the needs of Internet-based sales. We are willing to support Internet projects even if they take away sales from existing marketing channels. We can easily change the manner in which we carry out our tasks to fit the needs of the new Internet-based marketing channel. We can easily accumulate the necessary knowledge to be able to sell by use of the Internet. We are willing to sacrifice sales through our existing channel in order to stake on Internet-based sales. We are willing to pursue a new technology even if it causes existing investments to lose value.			
Firm size Mean = 138 S.D. = 454	Number of employees.			
Product complexity Mean = 13.4 S.D. = 4.1	Our products are too complex to be sold via the Internet. The customers often want a demonstration before buying our products. Our products are often adapted to the individual customers' special needs and wants. We discuss the products with our customers before they buy.			
Strong brand names Mean = 3.5 S.D. = 1.4	Our products are brand names.			
Payment difficulties Mean = 3.0 S.D. = 1.2	There is too much uncertainty connected with payment over the Internet.			

Scale format:					
1 **Strongly disagree**	**2** **Disagree**	**3** **Neutral**	**4** **Agree**	**5** **Strongly agree**	

Construct name:	Items used:
Contractual difficulties Mean = 3.0 S.D. = 1.2	It is connected with too much uncertainty to make contracts by use of the Internet.
Market maturity Mean = 5.9 S.D. = 2.1	The users of our products want to be able to buy by use of the Internet. The market is ready for Internet commerce.
Market uncertainty Mean = 7.9 S.D. = 2.9	Internet-based sales and marketing is too uncertain. It is difficult for us to determine whether Internet-based marketing channels will be a success. The effect of Internet marketing is too uncertain.
Competitors Mean = 4.3 S.D. = 2.1	Our closest competitors have started using the Internet for sales and marketing. We feel pressured to use the Internet because our competitors already use it.
Distributor reactions Mean = 14.7 S.D. = 5.6	Internet-based sales and marketing will lead to conflicts with our dealers. The dealers will lose trust in us if we start selling our products via the Internet. The dealers will find other products to sell if we sell our products via the Internet. Sales via the Internet will decrease sales in our other channels. If we start selling via the Internet our dealers will be unsatisfied.

Index

Index *139*